"Single in the City *is a brilliant, authentic and witty insight into the single world. Laura Bilotta shares tips and stories to find your ideal life partner. Follow Laura's expert advice and you won't be single for long!"*

~ **Carol Starr Taylor**,
Author, *Life in Pieces: From Chaos to Clarity*,
Inspirational Speaker, Life and Business Coach,
NLP Practitioner, Time Line Therapy Practitioner,
Hypnotherapist and the Founder of The Travelling Sisterhood

"I love a natural read. Laura Bilotta's real approach to matchmaking and her dating advice is exactly what singles need to navigate the messy world of dating. She shares her very real personal dating experiences, and the trends and key insights from her professional experience, in such a concise and simple way that you can't help but get better at dating after you dive into this book. Thank you, Laura, for sharing your wisdom so singles can live more fulfilling lives while on their quest for lasting love."

~ **Yvonne Sinniah**,
Relations Advisor and Founder of Love Inspired

"Single in the City *looks at common missteps people make in the dating process and shows how to do it right. It's an easy and witty read. The chapter about writing your dating profile is spot-on! Finally, someone is saying no more 'walks on the beach.' It's a great book for anyone wandering into the murky waters of online dating."*

~ **Dawn Maslar**,
Author, *Men Chase, Women Choose:*
The Neuroscience of Meeting, Dating, Losing Your Mind,
and Finding True Love

"Laura Bilotta's Single in the City *is a must-read for anyone having trouble finding a lasting relationship. Her insightful tips and savvy suggestions will help anyone re-evaluate who they are and what they are looking for in a mate. Though most people have a visual ideal in their minds, Bilotta reminds us never to judge a book by its cover and to peel off the skin and taste the fruit within. With a personal touch, and tidbits about her dating disasters and success, Bilotta makes us believe that 'The best relationships challenge you to grow and change to become a better you.'"*

~ Lisi Tesher,
Relationship Expert

"After reading Laura Bilotta's exciting book, I was left with the belief that if you want to attract the best, you have to be your best. Yes, it's finally here—a how-to book that will undoubtedly increase the likelihood of you finding the heterogeneous relationship you've been searching for. Laura gives us a blueprint for both genders who are seeking that someone special to share their life with. Most of us who seek companionship, intimacy and friendship want that relationship <u>now</u>. You will be able to read this book within hours and use the insights gained immediately. Laura covers the topic of dating from both a traditional and modern perspective, and also touches on timely topics such as Internet dating, speed dating and divorce. I highly recommend this book for anyone wanting to bring their best to their special relationship."

~ David Feder,
MSW, RSW,
Therapist, Close Connections

"Laura is a seasoned matchmaker and expert dating coach who has helped thousands of single men and women find their ultimate partners. Her new book Single in the City *takes you on a guided path to self-discovery and helps you to understand what you really want in a partner. Caution: Don't read this book unless you're ready to end your single status!"*

~ Dr. Antonio Borrello,
Psychologist, Relationship Therapist,
Author, *Dating 2.0*

"Laura's book is a must-have for anyone looking to get into a relationship or even improve the one they are in. Her tell-it-like-it-is style, authentic sharing of her own experiences and list of questions give the reader deep insight into themselves and prospective partners. After reading Single in the City, *I'm sure you won't be single for long."*

~ Priya Ali,
Coach/Consultant,
iTV Host/Executive Producer

"I highly recommend this book to both men and woman who are single and searching in the dating world today. Laura has some fantastic and insightful advice that is useful in everyday life. She uses her personal experiences to relate to the reader, while adding entertaining and thought-provoking client stories. I was very impressed with the content of this book and found it to be an enjoyable read. Single in the City *should definitely be on your list of must-reads and would make an excellent gift for any single loved ones."*

~ Kai Downes,
Relationship Consultant, The Love Listeners, Inc.

"Current and up-to-date with how to navigate as a single person in this decade of online dating and technology. Excellent references to the languages of love. I also am a true believer in knowing what ignites the meaning of love in oneself. I highly recommend this book to anyone who wants to learn and understand how to find the most compatible person, soulmate, ever-lasting love!"

~ **Lorelyn Martin**,
President & Founder, Lorelyn's Gourmet Desserts

"Laura writes from the heart through the sharing of her experiences. She brings you on a journey of self-discovery and helps you truly understand how to find the perfect partner."

~ **Giovanni Maccarrone**,
Toronto Life Coach

"I was always looking for love in all the proverbial 'wrong places.' I didn't know that I needed a dating coach … until I met Laura. She helped me realize that some of my dating direction needed a tune-up. I took her advice to the letter, and have since met my wonderful husband. Her new book is relevant, quotable, practical, doable and inspirational. Nowhere have I read such a comprehensive book about the highs and lows and ups and downs of dating. A must-read for those who are looking for love."

~ **Sandra**,
Dietician/Nutritionist,
Former Client

"I've been working with Laura for some time now and always value her tips and advice. When she gave me a copy of her book, I was happy to have a take-home reference that I could use as a reminder. It's an easy read, charming and witty, and has given me great insight into what I am projecting when meeting a woman for the first time. I highly recommend this book!"

~ Trevor,
Lawyer,
Former Client

"This book is jam packed with really good advice about finding the right match for you. When I was a client, Laura helped me see things in a different way. I came to realize that what I thought I wanted in a mate was not right for me. I am happy to say that I've taken her advice and am now in a loving, committed relationship. This book is filled with lots of great advice. It's like a well-written conversation with Laura. I'm planning on buying a copy for my recently divorced sister; I'm sure she will LOVE it too!"

~ Janet,
Business Owner/Entrepreneur,
Former Client

"I can say as someone who's been a partner, friend and client, Laura knows her s*it when it comes to relationships. After helping thousands of people find their match over decades of front-line, real-world experience, she has perfectly laid out what works in this book. Many find dating to be an overwhelming and confusing ordeal ... that will change after reading what's in Single in the City. *Her keen insights are to the point, relevant and more importantly, authentic."*

~ Patrick Power,
Corporate Headhunter
& Co-Host of the Single in the City Talk Show

Single In The City

Laura Bilotta lives her own beliefs as a dating coach!

Having experienced as many failed relationships as those who sought her help, including getting dumped by the "perfect" guy, she turned to Laura Bilotta, herself, to discover what was wrong in her own dating pattern.

Now a TV Host, author, and matchmaker, she came to the conclusion that all professional relationship advisers agree is the crucial: You have to know and like yourself before you can hope to know and like someone else. That's how Laura recognized that being dumped was really a favor given to her. He was the wrong guy for her because she was wrongly looking for superficial traits instead of the ones that matched her inner best self.

Laura's new book, *Single in the City,* reflects this experience along with her years of listening to others' dating woes and helping them learn to become the kind of person they'd want to date. And to accept that someone different from an idealized "perfect" mate may be the right match.

This book offers practical dating advice – even venturing bravely into assessing personal style with, "Do you really want to look like that?"

Single in the City is a natural addition to Bilotta's business model for teaching better dating skills, through her matchmaking site and speed dating events, along with her TV show. For singles wondering what more they can do to improve their chances for an enduring relationship, this book is another useful tool.

~ **Ellie Tesher**,
Syndicated Advice Columnist,
ellie@thestar.ca and ellieadvice.com.

Single in the City

Single in the City

From Hookups & Heartbreaks to Love & Lifemates:
Tales & Tips to Attract Your Perfect Match

LAURA BILOTTA

NEXT CENTURY
PUBLISHING

Single in the City
From Hookups & Heartbreaks to Love & Lifemates:
Tales & Tips to Attract Your Perfect Match

Published by Next Century Publishing
Las Vegas, Nevada

www.NextCenturyPublishing.com

ISBN: 978-1-68102-128-7
Library of Congress Control Number: 2016952983

Printed in the United States of America

INTRODUCTION

For more than fifteen years I've successfully coached and matched hundreds of singles, confident in knowing they were living happily ever after. Yet, here I was sitting in my kitchen, reflecting on many failed relationships of my own. They say those who can do, do; and those who can't, teach. But I knew I could both do and teach. I was capable of shifting my behavior and learning to apply my do's and don'ts of dating to my own life – wasn't I? However, it wasn't until I was dumped – yes dumped – by a man who made me believe, by dumping me, that he was the only man for me. This man was immune to my charms, my cuteness, my love of life. Of course, there was nothing wrong with him. It had to be me. This man was perfect, and I was desperate to get him back.

My aversion to rejection drove me. It drove me so hard, that I schemed and connived fantasies, wondering how I could manipulate him just enough, to give me one more chance. And when he never gave me that chance and dismissed my attempts, what did I do? I did what every normal person faced with rejection does. I cocooned. It took me years to truly get over him and I had to learn that compatibility is a core component in relationships, if love is going to be sustained.

Years later, I look back at this relationship and realize it could have been – would have been – toxic. Yes, he was muscular and athletic, and yes he was hot, but he was young and immature – and so was I!

Since that relationship, I've taken a closer look at who I am and who I want to be. The more I discovered about myself, the more I also realized I wanted to find a man who complemented me. I didn't need someone who groveled over me or catered to my every wish.

And I certainly didn't want to be that way either. I had been caught in that trap of making snap judgments – forming an opinion of a man based on his looks, and forgetting there was more to someone than "meets the eye."

I would figure this out – and I did!

You can too.

I am here to help you and that's exactly what I am going to do as you read this book. I'm going to help you take a good look at who you are – that's the first step towards knowing what type of person you want to be with. Then I'll help you understand and navigate through the dating world. Whether you are a man or a woman, the advice and direction offered in these pages will guide you in finding the right person for you. Hundreds of successful relationships are proof of this, including my own.

Happy reading!

Much love,

Laura

CONTENTS

SECTION 1
Know Who You Are

SECTION 2
Figuring Out Who And What You Want

SECTION 3
Gender Specific

SECTION 4
The Real World Of Dating

SECTON 5
From Dating To Relationship

SECTION 6
Early Relationships

SECTION 7
Dating After Divorce

Single in the City

Section 1

Know Who You Are

After years of being a dating coach, I have discovered one theme that stands out loud and clear from those who come to me. Each person is looking for compatibility and someone who meets their needs and makes him or her happy.

"What is wrong with that?" you might ask. "Isn't that what we are all looking for?"

Yes.

And no.

While I'm certainly not suggesting that you look for someone who makes you unhappy, the problem is you're focusing on the wrong thing. Relationships are not all about me, me, and me. Relationships are about two people being their best and contributing their best to each other. That means before you start looking for Mr. or Ms. Right, you have to *be* Mr. or Ms. Right.

In this section, I want to help you to understand yourself. Who are you? What are you really like? What are your innate needs? The more you find out about yourself, the more prepared you'll be to find a relationship that is truly right for you.

Be The One You Want To Date

$\mathcal{I}$t's late as you close your front door behind you. A smile spreads across your lips as you relive the delicious moments you've had that evening with your date. The warm feeling of fulfillment fills your body. After you slide into bed, sweet memories lull you to sleep.

Have you ever had one of those dates that went incredibly well? Unbelievably well. Your date was considerate, connected and fully present. He or she listened to every word you said as you both engaged in great conversation. Electricity darted back and forth. You thought, *This person is passionate, lives with purpose, and has the confidence to seize life and its opportunities.*

What the two of you experienced was the Law of Attraction in action. This law is a "New Thought" philosophy, a spiritual movement, that teaches "like attracts like." In short, it says your thoughts and energy, positive or negative, attract the same.

So how do you use the Law of Attraction to work in your favor?

First, let's take your ego out of the driver's seat. Instead, let your soul take control and always be "in the moment," believing only the best will come your way. When preparing for a date, consider what worked well in the past and think of the amazing experiences ahead.

I have heard many stories where the date went off course, often because of a misunderstanding, a misinterpretation, a defensive posture, or other such miscommunication. When this happens, we either become insecure because we're riddled with fear or we look to dominate. It is crucial to recognize that our ego takes control when we think we are not safe. When preparing for, and when you first meet your date, consider the following:

Be authentic. This is not always easy because it requires a certain level of vulnerability. Feeling vulnerable means you potentially getting hurt, but at the same time vulnerability affords us the best chance for success.

I interview many singles in my matchmaking practice and I often hear: "All the good ones are taken." "Men are just looking for one thing." "Women are too superficial." It makes little sense to point the blame directly on others, because I have news for you: You and only you are the reason you are single.

The law of attraction is in effect; you attract who you are. If you think negatively then you will attract more of what you don't want. When you think positively, you will attract more of what you do want.

Ask yourself this question: Would I date myself? If the answer is no, then you can't expect someone else to want to date you. Do you possess the qualities that others are looking for? Can you engage someone in conversation? Do you have good morals and values?

Are you:
- Intelligent?
- Loyal?
- Honest?
- Trustworthy?
- Kind?
- Optimistic?

- Interesting?
- Confident?
- Healthy?
- Passionate about life?

If the answer is "no" to most of these questions, then you really need to work on yourself to become the person whom you want to be with in a relationship. Being healthy and staying active are so important for your entire well-being, and that means working on yourself – mind, body and spirit.

If you think negatively then you will attract more of what you don't want. When you think positively, you will attract more of what you do want.

When you are fulfilled and content, you are at your best and you will attract positive experiences. When bad things happen you will be able to shrug them off more easily. You will also attract people who are in the same emotional state and on the same life path as you. This is when magic happens! A dynamic and hearty relationship is formed when two people, equally content and fulfilled, come together.

Become who you want to date.

I will repeat that again.

Become who you want to date.

Having an uncluttered emotional state before you start dating is important. Your past can really affect how you view your future. However, bad experiences are not an excuse for mistreating others or playing the blame game.

Just because someone cheated on you does not mean *everyone* will do the same. You are meeting new people, and you can't bring your baggage with you or any potential relationship is destined to fail. You have to be okay with what happened in your past. You have to learn from your experiences and move on. But how? There are a number of methods, but do stay away from voodoo dolls, hexes, poxes, and hitmen.

Those will only come back to bite you. You might want to see a counselor or therapist who can help guide you through these very important stages. Or you can turn to a trusted friend or family member. But l-i-s-t-e-n to whomever you seek out, especially if you are hearing the same thing from more than one person.

What I can tell you is that if you've been betrayed, lied to or cheated on in the past, it is important to do the work to get over the hurt and realize that not everyone is the same. If you fail to do this, you'll end up being like a hamster running on a wheel. You'll simply repeat your pattern. And you'll keep inviting the same kind of people who will hurt you.

After each relationship, step back and learn from it. What is it that went wrong? What went right? What was I putting up with? What was I willing to compromise on? What am I not going to put up with again? What will I put up with again? What am I looking for, and not looking for, in a future partner? Write down all the men or women you've had dates or relationships with, and next to their names, write what you liked and didn't like; and what did and didn't work. By doing this, you are creating guidelines for what you are looking for, and who you are looking for, in a relationship.

Different Can Be Good

As the founder and "face" of Single in the City, I've talked with hundreds of trustworthy strangers who have willingly accepted my well-reputed advice, and found a loving someone with whom to share their lives. But I struggled. I'd been on enough dates, and even had relationships that I thought were right for me.

Then along came Dean.

Dean is, well, different. He didn't have that hulking physique that triggered my primal emotion of submissiveness. In fact, he was what I considered to be *old*. I had always been attracted to younger men, more likely six years younger and not six years older like Dean. I believed relationships with older men were boring and lacked sustainability. But as I got to know Dean, I realized that age should be a consideration, but it should never restrict my dating pool. Dean and I have been together now for five years, and we have a wonderful relationship.

Like me, you may be stuck in a particular dating criterion, including age. So consider the fact that "different can be good!"

Yes, we all want Mr. or Mrs. Right to join us on the journey of a dream-come-true relationship. My goal is to help you find the right person for you. And that's your goal, too! So let's work together and figure this out – including being willing to look outside of your normal dating criteria.

Is He/She for Me?

Perfection. Isn't that what we are all looking for in a mate? The trouble is that there is no such thing as a perfect person – something I'm sure you're fully aware of. And what perfection means to one person, is not the same for another. We all have flaws that we often forget when sizing up others.

We are always looking for social acceptance and acceptance from others in how we look and act, so we have to practice what we preach *before* entering a relationship. If you want others to accept your flaws, then you have to accept the flaws of others. This can be difficult for some people.

When you're deciding if you should go out with him or her, there are many factors you'll consider. Age is one of them. Dating younger can work, as long as the individual is mature enough to handle a relationship and has an understanding of where he or she is going in life. However, a younger person might create unwanted volatility, as he or she navigates their way through life. Older men and women can be more mature, loving and relationship-worthy, but they can also be more set in their ways. So ask yourself, *What am I looking for in a relationship?* The answer to that question will go a long way in determining age-appropriate dates.

For instance, I met Dean after I had figured out my ideal relationship. And I was drawn to him before I ever saw him. I heard his laughter from a distance and it sparked my attention. There was just something about his voice that told me he had a zest for life.

As I got to know Dean, I realized what a kind, happy and uplifting man he was. Someone who was strong both mentally and physically.

Today, I can tell you that Dean is decisive, responsible and a real protector – the man who helps me be the best possible version of me. The man who lovingly gazes into my eyes, and tells me I am beautiful, even when I go to bed with wet hair and wake up looking like the Lion King.

My point is that I had been limiting my dating pool to men whom I thought were right. When I met Dean, I quickly found out that he doesn't need to spend hours primping himself in front of a mirror, making sure his hair is perfectly styled or his arms are shaved before anyone comes over (yes, I dated someone like that). He's secure in himself. He knows what he wants and gets things done. But I would never had known this about him had I not opened myself up to redefining my type.

There is always the possibility that your "type" might not be who you should be looking for. Sorry to bombard you with this, but I am trying to make a point about escaping the inevitable repetitiveness of your "comfort zone." But, if Muscle Man or Blonde Bombshell one-through-six didn't work out for the same re-occurring reasons, they may not be your ideal option moving forward; maybe the next person you consider dating should be ... different.

Not odd different, but a new kind of different. Here is my challenge: The next time someone catches your attention because of how they are—not only what they look like—take the time to get to know them. I'm not saying to dismiss physical attraction; I'm saying to be willing to look deeper at the person. This can be refreshing and you never know where it may lead.

For all you know, you may become absolutely smitten with that different individual. The one who lives down the hall and wears his socks up to his knees, or the woman you see every day at work, who hardly says a word to anyone. (Socks up to his knees ... is this guy for real? Actually, he might be.)

Let's consider Kali. Kali is in her early 40s and had become a slave to her preferences. This girl is attractive, successful, and is one of those women who easily makes others laugh and smile. She, however, had been single for more than two years. During that time, she focused solely on herself – achieving a stage in her career, and personal life that brought her happiness and contentment. The problem was that she had become so comfortable with being single, that letting someone into her life seemed like more of an imposition, and would probably involve compromises. Kali didn't like compromises. When we spoke, she insisted she didn't need my assistance. She knew exactly what she wanted and could find it on her own.

As she made her way back into the dating scene, she had many firsts, but no seconds. This, too, she insisted was her choice. It very well could have been, but she had turned into a serial dater, which tells me she was looking for the wrong kind of man.

She had a list of wants that she deemed needs: Successful, super-hot, 6'0" and over, great hair, strong conversationalist, a great sense of humor, physically fit; she would accept a 6-pack but preferred an 8. This was a compromise to her. She also wanted a man who loves sports and was not too clingy so she wouldn't have to sacrifice her independence.

Guys, you have your female equivalent of this person.

Well, everyone is looking for someone like that! But limitations such as these are a big reason why there are so many singles in our society.

Back to Kali. She finally got back in touch with me, with an open mind. First, we discussed her. Who she really is. Kali is a bit of a tomboy. She loves playing and watching sports and would rather spend a Saturday night with her male friends watching the big game than an evening with her boyfriend. She is very independent and often pays for first dates – she doesn't want to feel like she owes anyone anything. She lives in hoodies and jeans, and makes little effort when going out on a first date. What a shocker that tall, gorgeous, confident men with bodies like Adonis weren't pounding down her door!

We started discussing what she would be willing to overlook in a potential date. A couple of weeks later, she told me she had met a man through one of her weekly sporting activities, whom she was crazy about – and someone she wanted to see again and again. Marc was attractive – to her – successful, had a great sense of humor … and only 5'10". He was also bald, not quite as buff as she liked; he wasn't fat, he was…a little softer and rounder than she normally went for. As for the hair that was missing from his head? It was spread over the rest of his body. But the chemistry between the two was incredible and he was the first guy who gave her butterflies.

"I listened and finally *heard* what you said, and applied your lessons," Kali told me. "I stepped out of my comfort zone."

Are you stuck in the same trap as Kali? Are your more common forms of dating not working for you? Is Mr. or Ms. Familiar causing you problems? I encourage you to be like Kali. There is room for flexibility, and your list is more malleable than you might think.

You only have to slightly modify your list and you might do this without even realizing. You don't want to be trapped in the confines of predictability, and due to the repetitive behaviors of your "type," you might unknowingly be putting yourself into doomed-to-fail relationships.

The biggest problem with dating outside of your cozy confines is discomfort; this kind of exploring can leave you feeling a little uneasy, but the truth is it may not be as uncomfortable as you imagine. Maybe your taste in men or women has changed and you don't even know it yet. These things happen.

It might be that initial spark of chemistry that ignites your passion for someone, but that spark can easily turn into a full blown, destructive, soul-burning fire when the smallest of things goes wrong.

We tend to be attracted to partners who not only share the exciting and positive qualities similar to our own, but we are also drawn to people who possess similar *unfavorable* qualities. The ones we all wish we could sweep under the rug. Remember, you are who you attract.

A relationship isn't just about animal magnetism;
the best relationships challenge you to grow and
change to become a better you.

When you choose to try something different, chances are the outcome will be unfamiliar and exciting! And that new person may even challenge you in areas that you don't like about yourself. A relationship isn't just about animal magnetism; the best relationships challenge you to grow and change to become a better you.

"Variety is the spice of life," they say, yet I continue to notice that many people don't like a spicy life – or variety. This could be the secret to finding "the one."

What am I talking about, you ask?

When you open yourself to new possibilities, you'll be ready to explore a world of new love and potential.

Let's start here:

- Approach that person you've had an eye on at work or the gym.
- Go somewhere different, join a new group or explore new hangouts.
- Strike up a conversation with a stranger at the grocery store.
- Meet people you wouldn't normally at your neighborhood bar.
- Participate in activities you love.

Well before I met Dean, I had always been a shy woman when it came to speaking to a guy I found attractive. But I wanted to push myself and get comfortable speaking to strangers. So I decided to explore new opportunities by approaching men and suggesting a date. For instance, sometimes while shopping, I would catch sight of an attractive man in my periphery. I would scribble my phone number onto a piece of paper, hand it to him and say something like, "I'm Laura. If you don't have a girlfriend and would like to go for drinks sometime, give me a call." I put myself out there and more often than not, I'd get a phone call. I had nothing to lose. If he called, great and if he didn't oh well, maybe he didn't find me attractive or maybe he had a girlfriend. I would never really know so I didn't let it bother me. That was over five years ago. Nowadays, don't expect a call back but rather a text.

Imagine if Italian explorer Christopher Columbus had never voyaged across the Atlantic. No doubt he was comfortable in his native Genoa, Italy, and his first journey almost cost him his life! If his ship hadn't burned off the coast of Portugal, he never would have had to swim to the coast and find his first wife – in Portugal. Nor would he have discovered the New World. But, he stepped out of his comfort zone and put himself out there; as a colonizer, a businessman, he knew there was more for him to see.

You can be "Christine or Christopher Columbus," too - get out of that rut! Try different events, such as speed dating, socials, dances, business networking or trade shows.

Now go on, lace up your boots, throw on that
funky adventure gear, and start exploring!

With the people I've talked to recently I've realized that networking, whether through business, a social club, a church, or other venue, can be invigorating and rewarding. Here's why: When you meet new people you expose yourself to natural dating opportunities. Your new friend may not become the next object of your affection; it could be his brother or sister, their best friend, or that cutie who asks you out at the coffee shop right after your latest networking buddy pays their tab and hits the road. Love strikes when we least expect.

Now go on, lace up your boots, throw on that funky adventure gear, and start exploring!

BECOMING THE RIGHT PARTNER

*W*ouldn't it be great if we could all look like the gorgeous guys and women on the popular TV shows "The Bachelor" and "The Bachelorette"? Have you ever dreamed of being on these shows? Wouldn't it be amazing to have a plethora of people wanting to date you? (I'm not so sure I'd want to be one of those that are in the "herd".) Attraction. Passion. Romance. Perfect dates.

While TV shows such as these appeal dreams, the truth is they also create false expectations. Reality check #1: These shows take at least three months to produce. Those in the cast give up their everyday lives, and don't have to worry about the daily grind of life and all the issues that come with it. Sadly, after Mr. and Miss Bachelor/Bachelorette get together and begin spending time in the real world together, they often break up.

In my years of giving dating advice, I've noticed after the initial attraction wanes, there are two common denominators that can quickly doom a relationship: 1) People don't really understand themselves, so they don't know what strengths and weaknesses they bring to a relationship; 2) and men and women are searching for a relationship based on what they can get out of it, instead of what they can contribute.

People with holes in their soul attract people with
holes in their souls. But people who are whole
attract people who are whole.

Reality check #2: If you are not working on yourself, if you are not emotionally growing, maturing, and learning to handle your weaknesses, then you'll find a relationship through "selfish" eyes. Then, when the other person doesn't meet your expectations, or he or she does something that gets you upset, you'll be looking for the quickest exit.

A counselor friend of mine has a saying: People with holes in their soul attract people with holes in their souls. But people who are whole attract people who are whole. Experience tells me he is right.

Who Are You – Really?

With the aforementioned reality checks in mind, I'd like to help you understand who you truly are. In order to equip you with tools so you can walk a path towards finding the right partner, we must first delve into the multiple dimensions of temperament, love languages, compatibility and chemistry. When we approach our relationships with a fuller understanding of our own inner self, we can better identify who we really connect with. So let's take a look at:

- ❧ The 4 Temperaments
- ❧ The 5 Love Languages
- ❧ Chemistry versus Compatibility

The 4 Temperaments

Everyone is born with a particular temperament that dominates our lives. Our temperament determines the way we see life with the way we interact with people, and the way we interpret what is happening to us. Temperament is also the greatest determining factor whether we're an introvert or extrovert.

What does your temperament have to do with dating? Everything. While we all "put on our best face" during our initial dates, we also all eventually become the person we truly are as we move into the relationship. We do what comes to us naturally – good and bad. And the things we might not like about the other person – the things we "overlooked" during the first dates – really start to bug us. This is where disagreements and arguments begin to set in. Our temperament is clashing with Mr. or Miss "Right" and we don't even realize what's going on.

Psychologists have identified four defined temperaments types. While one of these will be dominant, we can operate in the other three, depending on the situation we find ourselves. As you go through the following chart ask yourself: Where do I fit in? What type of temperament and/or traits within the temperaments, are you typically attracted to or turn you off? What temperament most resonates with you and what temperament is secondary? Be as honest as possible with yourself as you read through.

1. **Sanguine**. These people tend to be fun-loving, optimistic, realistic, and focused on the here and now. They pride themselves on being unconventional, bold, and spontaneous. They make playful mates, creative parents, and troubleshooting leaders. Sanguines are excitable, trust their impulses, want to make a splash, seek stimulation and prize freedom. They are:

Influencing of others
"Super-extrovert"
Natural salesmen
Outgoing
Never at a loss for words
Doesn't like being alone
The "toucher," likes reaching out, touch is important to them
Messy lifestyle or overeating
Most emotional of temperaments
Bursts into tears or rage out of nowhere
Lacks self-discipline

2. **Choleric**. Are you a leader? Someone who takes charge? Someone who doesn't lose their head in a crisis? If so, then you are a Choleric. You are a dynamic, self-motivated person who can set your sights on a target and relentlessly pursue it until success is achieved. You are a strong-willed individual who makes decisions quickly and decisively, and who readily and easily grasps difficult concepts and strategies. Learning comes quickly to you, and you like to take action immediately. Choleric people are:

Decisive
Rational
Forceful
Active
Strong-willed
Independent
Opinionated
Thrives on activity
Practical
Sound quick decisions
Not afraid of obstacles

Strong natural leader
Does not display compassion easily
Details irritate them
Construction, supervision or coaching
Goal/task oriented
Anger, hostility, active temper, carry grudges, tells people off
Does not show public emotion
Emotions less developed
Inconsiderate
Opinionated

3. **Melancholy**. Time alone is vital for reflective, introspective Melancholy people. A perfectionist at home and on the job, they are likely the one with the perfectly organized closet and kitchen, the tidy desk-top, and the painstaking attention to following the rules. They long for a deep soul mate, yet when they are around people, they often find themselves mistrustful and disappointed. However, once committed to a relationship, they are unwaveringly loyal and self-sacrificing. They are:

Conscientious
Guardian
Introverted
Analytical
Perfectionist
Most moody
Can be antagonistic
Does not make friends easily
Most dependable
Prefers status quo
Doctors, scientists, writers
Highly self-critical

Easily offended
Feels persecuted
May seek revenge
Intolerant
Impatient

4. **Phlegmatic.** As a Phlegmatic, you have a dry wit and a steady, amicable demeanor. You are dependable, polite and even-tempered. You feel more comfortable in a small group of friends or even spending a quiet evening relaxing at home. You are rarely flashy or belligerent. You would rather take the blame (even unjustly) than stir up controversy or pick a fight. On the job, you seek neither power nor the limelight, but work steadily, patiently, and methodically. These people are:

Steady
Idealists
Calm
Not easily disturbed
Easy to get along with
Most timid
Uses humor to make points
More observer
Teachers, counsellors and administrators
Dependable, organized
Lack of motivation or laziness
Selfish
Stubborn
Fearful

I'm sure you can now see why understanding your temperament – and the temperament the person you want to date – is critical to your relationships. So what did you learn about yourself and your temperament? Did you jot down the temperament you're most attracted to? Do you have a pattern of dating a certain temperament or characteristics of a temperament that isn't working for you? I encourage you to go back over the charts a few times to better answer these questions.

The 5 Love Languages[1]

The words "love language" sound so romantic. Wouldn't it be great if you and the person you're dating truly connected? Wouldn't it be awesome if you could say, "He gets me." or "She knows what makes me tick." Well, if you know your love language, and that of the one you are dating, this type of connection can really happen.

Gary Chapman is the founder of the 5 Love Languages. His universally proven concepts show how love languages affect the depth of connection and communication within a relationship.

So what do the words "love language" mean? We all have an emotional love tank that needs to be filled up on a regular basis. It is what "fuels" your soul. When your love tank is full, you feel better about yourself and the world around you. You act more appropriately, talk in more even tones, you get along with others better, and even have more patience. Here's a practical analogy: You wouldn't expect to drive your car all week without filling up it, would you? If you didn't pull into a gas station periodically, eventually your car would stop working. Well, you and I are the same way. When our love tank is empty, we are cranky, crabby, and we refuse to "work" on our relationships.

Let's look at Gary Chapman's 5 Love Languages, so you can figure out what it is you need – and what the one you're dating, or looking to date, wants most from you.

---

1   Chapman, Gary, The Five Love Languages. Northfield Publishing, 1992, 1992, 2005.

Words of Affirmation

Someone, whose love language is words of affirmation, prefers spoken words of appreciation and praise. This means you want a partner who is open and expresses their love and appreciation of you. These are unsolicited comments and verbal compliments. For example, hearing: "I'm so glad that you're here tonight with me," would be music to your ears.

Acts of Service

Actions speak louder than words for you. It's important to feel love through action and to see the person you are with go out of their way to do kind things for you. These are even the smallest gestures. For example, you love it when your date surprises you after work to cook you dinner after a long day.

Receiving Gifts

Do you feel loved when you receive gifts? These are gifts that are not just on special occasions, but non-occasion days. It's the thought that counts and resonates with this love language. For you, when your partner returns from a long business trip you want to know that they were thinking of you. Part of that, is them bringing you a gift to show they took the time out of their schedule to think of you.

Quality Time

Spending time together is important to you. It's important to you to feel that your partner is fully present and engaged. You want their undivided attention when during this time. For you, this is when your partner puts their phone away and plans a night together, just you and them.

Physical Touch

Not to be confused with sexual desire, your love language is felt most through touch. You love holding hands and when your partner reaches out to touch you. You want to feel touch from your partner. When they grasp your hand, or touch your back, sparks of love are ignited within you.

What did you learn about yourself and the way you prefer to express and receive love? You might be saying, "I identified with all five!" I've heard that before and it always makes me chuckle. While it's true that we really do connect with all of these, here is a clue to figuring out what really fills you up: What do you naturally do for others? When talking to someone, do you pat him on the back or touch her shoulder? If so, you are a physical touch person. When someone is not feeling well, do you send them a get well card or offer to help in some way? Then your love tank is acts of service.

Although not having the same love language as your partner is never a deal-breaker, it's important that you know each other's love language. That way you can focus on what he or she needs. Now think about this: If you and your partner were focused on meeting each other's needs, wouldn't your relationship go much smoother? Here's something else to think about: When you're looking for the right one for you, if you find someone with the same love language as you, then you will naturally do for each other what you need the most – making this a win-win for the both of you!

What Is Compatibility?

You may be thinking, "If I understand temperament and love languages, then I'll automatically choose someone I'm compatible with." Yes and no. Yes, these two will make you more compatible, but when I'm talking about compatibility, I am referring to an alignment of lifestyle choices and values between two people. There is a sense of like-mindedness.

To be compatible with someone, you don't have to be identical, but your core values and beliefs, for the most part, need to be in line. For example, if one person is very spiritual/religious and the other is not, this may be a deal breaker. I encourage you to take a good look at what is really important to you. Are you career-minded? Do you value the environment? Are you sports-minded? Do you like country or city living? What about music, food, clothing? While it's important that you have your own views and opinions – you certainly don't want to date someone exactly like you; that would become boring – when you have interests and similarities, compatibility will be instantaneous and will deepen over time.

Chemistry, Anyone?

Chemistry is your emotional connection with someone. It's the "spark," or the attraction that draws you to them. Some people refer to this as "electric"; it's that jolt that runs through your body every time you are near them. It's the butterflies and feeling like you can't get enough of that person.

While compatibility can work without chemistry, chemistry cannot work without compatibility. If you have chemistry with no compatibility, the relationship can be quite tumultuous and volatile.

The truth is, in the right partner, you want a mix of both chemistry and compatibility. To find the best mix of that for you, ask yourself:

- ⊛ What types of people are you most compatible with?
- ⊛ What types of people do you date? What is working for you, what is not?
- ⊛ What are your deal breakers?

What personality and temperament spark chemistry for you in someone?

What do you want in a partner?

Ultimately, compatibility and chemistry come down to that "feeling" someone is right for you. Your intuition will never steer you wrong, trust it. You don't have to agree on everything, but compatibility and chemistry will bring out the best possible version of both of you. You love and respect each other's similarities and differences. The right person for you IS out there. Now that you know more about yourself and the type of partner you're looking for, go get them!

While compatibility can work without chemistry,
chemistry cannot work without compatibility.

Chapter 4

Learning To L-I-S-T-E-N

"Quit yelling and I'll listen to you."

"Well, if you wouldn't yell, I wouldn't shut down."

Have you heard those words before? Have you said them before? What's going on here? There's a communication breakdown.

To state the obvious, men and women communicate differently. Consider these scenarios:

A.) A group of women are having a party and the conversations are continuous. They complete each other's sentences. They identify with each other's emotions. Multiple conversations are going on at one time, and everyone is enjoying themselves.

B.) A team of guys have just finished their ball game. They gather for beers and pizza, and ridicule and complement each other over their play. They're having a good time with smiles and laughter all around.

When it comes to understanding how men and women communicate, there is a basic rule that applies: Women talk to relate, while men talk to report.

Men & Women: How We Communicate

Communication is an important part of a relationship, so much so, that when your communication breaks down, so does your relationship. We know that dating and relationships can be "work" at times, but being aware of the differences between men and women, and how we communicate, can decrease misunderstandings and foster empathy and consideration.

Using the examples below, let's take a closer look at how communication styles differ between men and women.

  "How could you not know?"

As connectors and feelers, women have a tendency to assume that men know exactly what they're thinking and need. Men on the other hand, communicate in a much more straightforward way through direct requests. It's important to understand that men are not mind readers and unless the woman communicates her needs, he's not playing a guessing game with her. In order to meet in the middle, the best approach is for the woman to be open about her feelings and not make any assumptions about what the man may or may not know.

"Do you remember the amazing song that was playing in the background the first time we met?"

Women have a striking memory for details especially when it comes to relationships, whereas men do not. Be conscientious and understand that just because a man can't recall all the details, does not mean he doesn't care for the woman.

⑨ *"This is what you should do."*

When it comes to solving problems, men are entirely solution oriented. A man's main focus is to give the woman advice and solve the problem as quickly and effectively as possible. This approach by the man can seem cold to a woman who is seeking compassion and advice. To meet in the middle, it's important for a man to approach a woman seeking help with sensitivity first, and then approach the problem. For women, it's important to offer help first then follow with sensitivity when it comes to men.

⑨ *"I just need some time to myself."*

One of the biggest misunderstandings when dating or in a relationship is when a man feels the need to retreat. Men seek solitude in order to solve problems and deal with their emotions, whereas women crave communication in order to process their emotions and let it go. Women often perceive the retreat of a man as a threat to the relationship because of her difference in communication style. In order to meet in the middle, as a woman, it's critical to provide the man enough space to work through his problem. On the male side, it's important for the man to show interest and compassion towards the woman. Ask her how she's feeling and be available to talk through the problem with her.

⑨ *"Why are you always bringing up the past?"*

Women connect everything, while men compartmentalize. What this means is that men like to focus on one thing at one time. Women on the other hand are multi-taskers and connect every dot from the past. For men, when a woman tries to talk about the past, it's only because she is connecting one event to another.

ⓥ *"Hello? Are you listening?"*

Women love to communicate and talk, and sometimes leave men on the receiving end. It's critical that a woman sees and feels she is being heard. That could be a simple nod or acknowledgement within the conversation. On the woman's side, it's important to not to talk over your man. Create space and pause for him to contribute to the conversation.

ⓥ *"He hardly shows he loves me."*

Women prefer reminders and affirmation that their men love and care for them. These don't have to be grandiose gestures, this could even be cooking her dinner after a long day of work or telling her how great she looks today (refer to the 5 Love Languages). Where a man assumes a woman still remembers his nice gesture from two months ago, a woman needs a bit more reassurance and affirmation.

To ready yourself for your dream relationship, it's important for both genders to be able to meet in the middle, to have compassion for communication differences and work through them in order to anticipate and respond appropriately to their partner's needs.

Figuring Out Who And What You Want

*Y*ou now have a good understanding of how you are, what makes you tick, and what makes you feel fulfilled. Now it's time to start preparing to change your status from single to "in a relationship."

In this section, I want to help you figure out what you want in a relationship and who you want to be with in a relationship. That should be easy, right? Given our emotional makeups, our personal likes and dislikes, and our thoughts about what makes a great relationship, this isn't as easy as it sounds. But the following chapters will go a long way in helping you determine the right relationship.

Chapter 5

Dating Basics

Are you ready? It's time to wade into the dating pool. But we are going to do this a little at a time. There is much to know, and the more you know the more confident you'll feel. On a first date, they say it takes only fifteen minutes for a man, and less than five minutes for a woman to determine if a second date is in the future. So let's get you prepared.

In this chapter, we'll look at an overview of the singles scene, which will help you begin to navigate through it to find the one who is right for you.

Dating 101

After talking to so many people, I'm still shocked at the lack of "dating etiquette" that exists. Call me old fashioned if you will, but there's something to be said for men and women who look good, dress respectably, have manners, show respect, and don't have foot-in-mouth disease. So let's start with some basics.

☙ Do You Really Want to Look Like That?

Consider your basic appearance, including your hair, skin, teeth and breath. Sure, you love your crazy color hairdo or your dreadlocks, and that's good! But extravagant hairstyles will always "limit your audience." So when you walk out that door, make sure your hairstyle doesn't look like you got a two-for-one at the dog groomers. Next, let's consider the first thing everyone will see – your face. As a woman, you may not be into makeup, or you may be a pro at prettying yourself up. Men, you may like yourself with facial hair or that smooth look. Whatever your style, neatness counts – trust me on this. While the scruffy beard look is a hot look for men these days, do you really need to look like you walked off the set of Duck Dynasty? Women, does the color of the blush and eye shadow you've chosen really complement you, or are you just trying to make a "statement"? How you look is up to you, but you may also turn off the very person you're interested in meeting.

I realize this all sounds very superficial, but the fact is we make snap judgments based on appearances – everybody does. It's our natural process of elimination; some things do not appeal to us, so we automatically eliminate anyone with those traits from our mental list of prospects.

Take Brian for example. He wanted to sign up for my matchmaking services. He told me that he often has sex with this "hot young chick," but was looking for a relationship. I found this a tad hard to believe because, well, Brian had virtually no teeth. He told me this hot chick, who was his boss's daughter, didn't care about his lack of teeth; she had sex with him anyways. I resisted the urge to tell him her motives were probably about pissing Daddy off, but that was none of my business. Although it did make it harder to convince him that I could not match him with anybody until he dealt with his missing teeth.

Brian said, "Yes, yes, I will, but that will take months. In the meantime, can you just set me up with someone, anyone, for now? I'll pay you more money."

I bit my tongue, because I have the tools to do that. Instead, I assured him that more money wouldn't change anything, and he should use that extra money and put it where his mouth is. I'm not sure he fully grasps the concept of matchmaking, but there was nothing more I could do for dear Brian. It's up to him. He has the ability and the means to be the best version of himself, he just needs to make the choice.

Finally, there's a need to address personal hygiene. To both guys and gals I say: Don't think that just because you've come from the gym, your hot-and-sweaty look is going to be attractive. And don't think that just because you've come from work and you are dressed fine, that you also smell good. Check yourself out: Do you need deodorant? A dash of perfume or cologne? Is your breath fresh? Be sure you're in the habit of brushing and flossing often. And limit the amount of garlic and onion you eat, especially raw. When you're in a crowded place and you're not sure if your breath is good, chew a piece of gum. Actually, just do all the above. We can't always smell our own smell, and determining whether or not our aroma is pleasant is not a task you want to delegate to someone else, especially if that someone else is the person you're interested in. It's a hard thing to come back from, it sticks with you, you know, like a bad smell.

Are You Really Wearing That?

In our society, there is a free-for-all when it comes to appearances: Anything and everything goes. That's okay, but I want you to think about something—how you dress says a lot about the way you think. For instance, guys, if your shirt is half hanging out your pants and your shirt smells like your laundry hamper, what are you telling that cute gal you have your eye on? She probably thinks your Mom does your laundry and you owe her a visit. Ladies, if you're always wearing sweats, you're only going to attract jocks and guys who aren't looking for anything long term. Sure, there are some days when leaving the house with sweats is justified, but if you're honest with yourself, most of the time you don't feel good about yourself when you do, and you're actually hoping you don't run into a cute guy.

Whether you're getting ready to go out on your first date or considering who to date, look at yourself first in the mirror after you're dressed and ask yourself, *Would I be attracted to me wearing this?* Remember not to hone in on the zit you know is there, nobody else can see it. Also, ladies, don't be afraid to wear a dress once in a while and embrace your femininity. Guys love a woman who can dress up, and in the summer it's so much easier to throw a dress over your head. Bonus points for those pretty, flowing dresses that are so forgiving on those I-feel-fat days we all have.

Yes, you have to be comfortable in your clothes, but your choice of clothing tells the opposite sex a whole lot about you – and you don't even have to say a word. Buy yourself some nice clothing so you can look great, but more importantly feel like you look great. You know what they say: "It is not what you wear, it is *how* you wear it."

First Impressions

I can hear you now: "I dress just fine, I look my best, and I smell good. So why can't I move past the first date – or even the first meeting?"

One, two, three, four, five, six, seven. That's how many seconds you have to make a first impression on someone. When you walk into a room and catch someone's eye, they've already decided if you are datable – and you have done the same. The way we walk, sit, or stand, our facial countenance, our smile or lack thereof, and many other deciding factors make up that initial seven seconds. So think about what you're portraying to others, and what someone is portraying to you. Before you walk into the room, take a deep breath, check yourself; (a) Do I have to pee? (b) Is my stomach okay or is it possible a fart is imminent? You know the drill. If all checks out then smile, stand up straight, look where you're going and walk over confidently while repeating, "this is going to be a fabulous evening" – though not out loud, because that sends a whole different message.

Be Date-Ready

I get it: You're ready to become un-single. So you must prepare yourself for dating and eventually for life in a relationship. Here's an easy place to start: Ask yourself, "*Why* am I still single?" (Notice the emphasis on why!) Here are some things to consider:

Are you going on dates?

- ⊛ Are you actually leaving the house?
- ⊛ Have you curbed the knee-jerk reaction to flip the bird at the honk of a horn?
- ⊛ Are you under 65 and have holes where teeth should be?
- ⊛ Are you going on dates?
  - ↬ Are you approachable? Is your wardrobe well put together? Do you have a positive attitude? Are you "on the lookout"? You never know when an opportunity will come knocking.
  - ↬ Are you a complainer, or someone who spends all their time whining about life and love? If this is you, then figure out why you are this way. Then decide you are going to change your outlook. Be positive, and find ways to have fun.
  - ↬ Do you live a healthy and physically-active life? Doing so will give you greater confidence and people will feed off your positive energy – you'll be more attractive and appealing. Not only will you get in shape and have more energy – you'll also have a great

opportunity to meet more people: You'll find a lot of singles at the gym; look for the ones who aren't glued to the mirror!

Don't be Afraid to Ask

As a date coach and matchmaker, I always tell my clients to ask their friends, co-workers or family to help them find a romantic partner. Someone in your personal network might have the perfect match for you, but maybe they don't say anything because you have never asked them. Or maybe those in your network think you prefer being single because, well, you are always single. Change that perception. Let your friends and family know that you're looking to change your relationship status. Then be prepared for some surprises.

Expand Your Social Circle

Asking others to help you find someone is great, but the responsibility still lies with you. Now, I'm not saying that you should walk the streets and talk to every stranger, but when you do go out, be friendly approachable. Spark a conversation with someone in line at the store or while sitting at the bar. Remember that one person you meet, though not ideal for you, can lead to meeting someone else, and that someone else might be the match you seek.

Smile, Smile and Smile

Remember what I said about making a first impression? A smile is one of the best ways to make that first connection. When you smile, people smile back. When you smile, you make it easy for others to let their guard down, which can quickly lead to a conversation. And once the talking begins, you never know where it will lead.

Use Dating Platforms

Dating has become so much easier with social media, speed dating, online dating/phone apps and more at your disposal. However, I've heard from many people that receiving an unsolicited "Hi, how are you?" from a stranger on Facebook is creepy and very invasive.

A matchmaker can be great for people who don't have a lot of time to get out and socialize on a regular basis and sift through thousands of profiles. Matchmaking sites, such as Single in the City, offer a portal for people to meet others with specific qualities and personality traits. We offer advice to step up your game and do the work for you. Hear me on this: By no means are you considered desperate if you use any one of these dating platforms; almost every single person is using or has used one or the other. Besides, this is the wave of the future for forming new relationships, so you might as well strap yourself in and get ready for the ride until you find "the one."

Speed Dating

Speed dating is a great way to get out and surround yourself with others who are single and looking. Believe me; nobody knows the speed dating industry better than me. I've been hosting Single in the City events for fifteen years and I've overseen countless connections. They are not free to attend, therefore, you're going to meet people who are more serious about wanting a relationship. These events are a great place to make new friends and explore possibilities!

Now don't be shy: Explore every opportunity that exists. Expand your social circle by any means necessary, because the more people you meet, the more likely you are to meet the right person for you.

In a culture where it has become increasingly harder to meet that special someone, speed dating adds a new possibility to finding true love. Speed dating events provide a platform to meet eligible, professional singles that you may not otherwise have the opportunity to meet face-to-face. It's great for people who have busy lives, who don't have a lot of single friends, who are tired of the bar scene, who have a difficult time approaching the opposite sex, who are new to an area, or those who want to brush up on their dating and conversation skills.

When you meet someone face-to-face, you generally know within a couple of minutes if there is chemistry between the two of you. You have the opportunity to meet 12-20 potential matches in one night, and the worst case scenario is that you end up having tons of fun and making new friends.

One of the biggest questions people ask me is, "What type of people speed date?" I always tell them: people just like you and me, people who are serious about meeting someone they want to spend the rest of their lives with.

I understand that people can be skeptical about who comes to these events. I also know that the media tends to portray speed dating events with "characters" that appear to have no hope of finding a relationship or are "weirdos." Don't let television be your barometer; it just isn't the case – it just makes good TV. When you go to a bar or to an event, are you attracted to every guy or girl in the room? No, of course not and the same goes for speed dating. You're never going to be attracted to everyone, but all you need is one person to stand out and who knows? They might just be for you.

All kinds of great people attend speed dating events and you never know just when that special person of your dreams will show up. I've seen people attend quite a few events with no luck and then bang, after a few more attempts, they finally meet the person they've been waiting for.

Most speed "date" times range from 3-5 minutes long, which is long enough to see if you the two of you have initial chemistry. The company that is hosting the event will exchange information between those interested in each other twenty-four hours later. So privacy is ensured.

Give It a Try

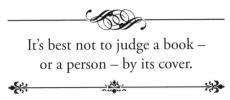

It's best not to judge a book –
or a person – by its cover.

In some instances, people have been so shy, I have found them at the front door, struggling with if they should stay or go. Others want to leave because they've scoped the room and figured they didn't like anyone there based solely on appearance. But remember, when you're skeptical about being somewhere your mind almost plays tricks on you like you're convincing yourself that you shouldn't be there and nobody will be suitable. After kindly persuading these individuals to give speed dating a shot, they actually thanked me for the wonderful experience. I've seen these same people come back again. At the end of the night, when I went to look at their cards to see who they chose, they had four or more picks. Lesson learned. It's best not to judge a book – or a person – by its cover.

Minor Adjustments

If you've been on countless dates, or had a few relationships, but nothing seems to last, then let me ask you something: Is it possible that you're looking for the wrong type of person? You know, the kind you quickly fall for at first sight, but soon realize they will never benefit society, and they're just happy in their oblivious lives?

That kind of person.

What's going on? Why do you fall for Mr. or Ms. Wrong all the time?

You feel like you're a pretty good catch. You are highly marketable, gainfully employed, friendly and you have turned a few heads in your time. What is holding you back from finding your soulmate?

I have encountered countless singles who can't seem to figure out why they have so much trouble with relationships or can't get past the first date. However, more often than not, you only need to make some minor adjustments to your approach.

For example, one of my clients, we'll call her Sarah, was on a dating journey and seemed to hit a wall. She is what I call a serial dater. Quantity versus quality. There was certainly no shortage of men she wanted to date, but she always found herself on a familiar path: She could never close the deal.

When Sarah came to me, she was frustrated, and we got right down to business. I started by having her look at her choices. Are you too picky? Are you looking for qualities and traits in a person who is out of your league? Are you being reasonable with your wants and needs? Maybe you're counting on Prince Charming riding in on a white horse and whisking you away? If that's your Plan A, it's time to move to Plan B.

Sarah had never considered her choices in this manner. Actually, she hadn't given her choices much thought at all, until now. I suggest you do the same. Be reasonable about whom you are looking for and you'll be amazed at the great people you'll end up meeting.

Smokin' Hot!

*H*ave you ever felt drawn to someone – even really liked them – but they weren't exactly what you were looking for? Or, more specifically, they didn't look exactly look like someone you *normally* dated, or someone others thought you would date. Or how about this: You date that person for a while, but the feeling of not matching up doesn't go away. You feel you are prettier or better looking, and he or she isn't acceptable in your eyes. What will people think? What will they say? This muttering in your head causes you to be so fixated on their looks, and you just can't get past your self-imposed roadblocks.

Here's another scenario: You are divorced and you've probably been on your own for quite some time. I don't just mean after the marriage has ended, but also in the weeks, months and perhaps years leading up to your divorce. So you are now "out there." You may have ventured to a bar or a social event with your friends. Then he walks into the room for the first time, and your eyes light up as your stomach does flip flops. Or, it's the first time she's entered your favorite pub, and your jaw drops while your heart races. Then he or she glances over at you and smiles, and you suddenly can't even think of your own name. It's called physical chemistry. Animal magnetism.

For most people, the initial physical attraction is what draws them to another person. While we all have our own preferences for what draws us, there is no denying the role that someone's looks play in our initial infatuation.

However, I've seen something happen more often than not. After a few dates when the initial attraction wears off, there is no more connection. Why? Because the two people have little in common. You might be thinking, *That won't happen to me.* But can easily happen if you succumb to the shallowness of your ego, and you are only looking for a "trophy" to have on your arm when you're out in public. *Please* don't fall into the trap of holding onto a looker with no personality, or issues that span the world.

You may find someone that you are very physically attracted to is emotionally unavailable. This is not a good match for you. The color of his hair, or lack thereof, size of her breasts, or the car they drive can quickly become irrelevant. Maybe this person had little to share, was too shy, couldn't make you laugh or even smile. But you were so sure the chemistry was there. Why? Because they were hot?

Here is something to keep in mind: *Finding someone attractive does not mean they are right* for you.

Most of the time, physical attraction is the first thing we notice. However, what is attractive to one person may be a turn off to someone else. Having said this, I encourage you to be a little flexible when it comes to looks. You'll be surprised what people, who are not driven by egos and the need to be admired, can offer.

Finding someone attractive
does not mean they are right for you.

Maybe he or she is not working with the greatest genetic material but the best thing is that most people who lack in the looks department can have a surplus of personality.

You have to be sensible. Real relationships are not "made in Hollywood" where Beast finds his Beauty or the princess kisses the frog. If you see a frog, it's just a frog – don't kiss it! The truth is that most people date at their "own level" because this is natural. But if you are looking for your fairy tale ending, re-read a couple of them, Sleeping Beauty spent her best years in a coma, Rapunzel spent hers locked away in a tower and Snow White's Step-Mother wanted her heart on a stick! So, let it go. Like really, let it go.

Attraction is not based solely only looks. Primal magnetism can be created by someone's passion, confidence, ability to communicate and overall personality.

Society is so superficial and we've been trained to believe what we see on the outside matters more than anything else. It's all about appearance. Sadly, we too often subscribe to the belief that we have to look a certain way, and date someone who looks a certain way. Otherwise we feel judged. But, if you like who you are dating – if you are truly attracted to that person – then why are you considering throwing away a potential relationship that makes the both of you happy? I challenge you: Get over the voice in your head and see that special guy or gal for whom they really are.

When I was dating, this has happened to me a lot. In 25 years of dating, I always based my choices on how good looking the guy was, and the ones who did not reach my standards were overlooked. Sadly, when I started to look into Mr. Hotbod's heart, I was shell-shocked. I would see he was really insecure, a self-absorbed control freak, and suddenly he wasn't so hot.

In my matchmaking business, I find many men and women who are still single because they insist on only dating within their "type." I am curious to know what factors are considered when determining this formula.

It is universally accepted, and known, that men place more importance on appearance. Women, on the other hand, are drawn to power. Why?

According to Psychology Today, there are many studies that show the preference of a woman's partner shifts according to their menstrual cycle.

The publication notes:

During peak levels of fertility, they prefer more masculine and socially dominant men. In the article these men are known as "cads." Indeed, they tend to be sexy, with their narrow eyes and strong jaws – but they also tend to be flashy and exploitative of others. Even worse, these masculine men often embody the Dark Triad, a personality constellation that encompasses Machiavellianism, psychopathy, and narcissism. Typically, these men offer only short-term prospects.

By contrast, during less fertile phases women are drawn to more feminine and compassionate men. These men are referred to as "dads." They tend to be more reliable, warm, and faithful than their caddish counterparts. They also offer greater prospects for a long-term relationship.[1]

What does this mean? The hot ones are not necessarily the right ones! Or, if you are serious about finding a good man, do so when it's not that time of month.

---

1   https://www.psychologytoday.com/blog/head-games/201308/what-women-want-in-men

Psychology Today, What Women Want in Men by Vinita Mehta Ph.D., Ed.M., August 5, 2013

Guys, I have not forgotten about you. Keep in mind that many hot babes are emotionally unavailable as well. They are stuck on themselves and the attention they draw when they walk into a room. Women like this are used to the attention and they crave it.

Think for a minute about how many partners those good looking guy and gals may have slept with. It is true when they say: You are sleeping with every partner your partner has ever slept with. Are you trying to figure out, now, how many secondhand partners you have had?

By no means do *all* attractive men and women fall into this category.

You need to know what you want and then go out and look for it. And when you see someone you want, go after them, or someone else will. That's why they say, *the good ones are gone early because the smart girls are not going to let the good ones get away.*

Consider these conversations:

Friend #1: "Are you dating someone?"

Dating Man: "Yeah I am dating this girl but she's not someone I would normally date; you know she's about forty pounds overweight." Or: *"She's a great girl and does all this stuff for me, but she's just not that hot."*

Friend #2: "Hey, who was that guy I saw you with the other day?"

Dating Woman: "We met a few weeks ago. I really like him, but his red hair is kind of a turn off." Or: *"He takes good care of me, but he's a little too skinny for my liking."*

Why does this have to be mentioned? Why can't you just say: "I am dating this great guy or gal, and…." Look beyond the initial attraction and you might be surprised by what you find.

People have been falling in love – sight unseen – over the phone, Internet or even in dark rooms, for decades now. Perhaps you have heard of a once unprecedented study, aptly titled *Deviance in the Dark,*

1973, by Swarthmore College, a liberal arts school in Pennsylvania.[2] Three social innovators, Kenneth J. Gergen, Mary Gergen and William Barton, sought to study the reaction of a group of students who were trapped together in two rooms; one fully lit and the second, a padded, pitch black room, 10'x12', the ceiling an arm's length above. They received no prior photos of the other participants, and initial contact was made by the sound of their voices.

Aside from the obvious claustrophobia, the groups of eight strangers – half male, half female, aged 18 to 25 – formed an unexpected bond. In fact, 90 percent of those in the dark room intentionally touched others in the room, while almost none of the light room participants made that same move. What's more 80 percent of respondents in the dark room said they felt sexual excitement, and some took it one step further and acted up on these tensions, kissing and touching those of the opposite sex before they were tapped to leave the room.

The report noted: "The fact that participants knew they would never meet face-to-face provided a final guarantee that they could interact in the way they wanted to… With the simple subtraction of light, a group of perfect strangers moved within approximately 30 minutes to a stage of intimacy often not attained within years of normal acquaintanceship."[3]

What this means is that people can find comfort, solace, and even share an attraction with someone they don't know and can't see.

To qualify the results of this experiment, the test was repeated with 22 more people.

Same outcome.

To draw a parallel, let's say online dating, and online dating sites, are the "dark room." No real visual contact, except for a photo, maybe two, plus a well-crafted profile. Sometimes factual sometimes well fabricated. (If you have been online dating for some time, you might have already experienced some elaborate fiction.)

---

2   Deviance in the Dark http://www.swarthmore.edu/Documents/faculty/gergen/
     Deviance_in_the_dark.pdf
3   See above reference

Example: *Daniel looked like a model in his profile photos. 6'4",
dimples and a banging body. When Tracy saw a message from him sitting
in her inbox, with his beautiful photo attached, she was elated. He was
so dreamy! Daniel's messages to her were well written; he was witty
and deathly charming. He even sent her additional photos – from his
"portfolio" – to further lure her. He freely provided his full name, which
she diligently used to research this guy. Daniel seemed perfect. He was
a working actor and had a few parts in some movies. He really was all
that – and a bag of chips. He had even been a model for a popular gym;
of course he would be just as gorgeous in real life...right?*

*Daniel and Tracy spent less than one week chatting online before
arranging their first date. Both of them were veteran online daters, and
neither wanted to play the pen pal game. Tracey was excited about him.
She eagerly watched the clock, counting the minutes until it was meet
time. Dinner and drinks with Prince Charming; it was just too good to
be true. But when Prince Charming showed up, Tracey almost choked
on her water. Daniel looked like he had swallowed Prince Charming for
lunch. He was big. The kind of big that you orbit.*

*Daniel failed to mention the few extra pounds he had inherited long after
the photos were taken, which wasn't very wise. If prepared, one is less likely
to audibly gasp upon laying eyes on you, and seriously, who wants to be on
the receiving end of that blow? Being a health freak, Tracy was disappointed.*

*But she honored her commitment and spent some time with him.
Tracy even ended up seeing him a couple of times over the weekend. He
was charming and kind, and their time together developed to the stage
that his smile made her melt.*

*Despite his looks, Daniel turned out to be a great guy. While it never
grew into anything long-term, Tracey was happy for the experience and
for meeting a man she now considers a close friend.*

Perhaps you have experienced this yourself.

Maybe he's not your Prince Charming. Physically, he might first
seem like he's wearing some kind of girl repellent. But then you get

to know him. So be open-minded because you never know who will come into your radar.

The Flip Side

Let's say you are totally attracted to someone. But there's a "maybe," or "I am not sure," lingering in your mind. This could be your intuition trying to tell you something. Perhaps you instinctively know there are traits about him or her that won't appeal to you; maybe it is a personality thing. Pay attention to your gut feelings; they could be a symptom of other things about that person that you will find unappealing. However, someone might not be the best looking, but once you fall in love with him or her they become better looking.

The bottom line is this: Yes, looks are important and they are a big part of chemistry. However, if you are solely focused on how "hot" someone is, you may be sadly disappointed in the quality of the relationship in the long run. And a disappointing relationship is something you're trying to avoid!

Chapter 7

Negotiables And Non-Negotiables

$\mathcal{C}$hoices. Likes and dislikes. Things we will compromise on. When it comes to dating, everyone has their preferences in looks, personality, and so much more. I call these negotiables and non-negotiables. What are your "must haves and turn offs" and the things that are not so important to you? Negotiables are not deal breakers; they are issues you can live with. Non-negotiables are issues you will not compromise because these go deeply against your values. A negotiable is something that does not offend your sense of integrity, but a non-negotiable does.

Before you even consider dating, you must take a good look at yourself. If you are carrying quite a bit of extra weight, don't expect Mr. Muscles or Miss. Model. If you are unemployed, or "transitioning," don't expect the CEO of the S&P 500. If you are a couch potato with nothing more exciting in your life than video games or the next episode of your favorite reality show, don't expect a biathlete.

It is good to have standards, but if you're going to be extremely picky, I guarantee you that you'll miss out on meeting some fantastic people. How long should your lists be? That's up to you, but be as as specific as you can with your non-negotiables so that you fully understand why these are so important to you. However, don't have a list down to your ankles because you'll never find an individual who meets all your requirements.

Example: *I met a lady at a Single in the City speed dating event, who then called me to inquire about my matchmaking service. The 41-year-old Muslim woman told me she wanted a family and was looking to marry a Muslim man to appease her mother's wishes. Well, her mother didn't have to sleep with him, so I told her she was compromising her happiness in exchange for her mother's and I asked her to consider what would happen when mom was no longer around. But she was adamant that she wanted a Muslim man with a great income and career. I searched through my database of singles and found a good match, but he was younger at 38. This was not a problem for her, but unfortunately, like many men, he was looking for someone younger than himself. Surprisingly, after hearing this, her demands became even more specific – and quite impossible. He had to be from the islands. Not African but specifically from the Caribbean, Jamaica preferred. He must already be rich. He must be taller than she, in excellent physical shape … her list went on and on.*

As I listened to her, I realized we were going nowhere. She even argued with me, saying that she knew it was possible, because she had recently been to Jamaica and saw a sign on the road that said: "Follow Me" referencing her religion. She should have followed that sign because there was no way I could help someone with such rigid criteria. Though I have managed to overcome many hurdles, that definitely required God-level miracle making.

If you often dismiss partners because your list is unreasonable, then you need to loosen up your rules. Be a little more adventurous and get to know someone before you unjustly judge them.

If possible, keep your list at five needs and five wants. Be strict about the must-haves; make no concessions when it comes to your beliefs and values. However, you may realize that even though you prefer a man over 6 feet or a woman with dark hair, maybe you can be open to meeting someone outside of whom you would normally consider. As well, don't compromise if you're truly not willing to accept someone's lifestyle. For instance, if having pet hair on furniture is a turn off, or you have pet allergies, it's almost a guarantee that pets will be an issue somewhere down the road. So don't make "mental concessions" that go against your values.

Let's explore some of the more common non-negotiables and negotiables.

If you often dismiss partners because your list is unreasonable, then you need to loosen up your rules. Be a little more adventurous and get to know someone before you unjustly judge them.

NON-NEGOTIABLES

Religion

Yes, there are far more important things in a relationship than theistic philosophies, but a conflict in beliefs can cause a lot of stress, if one partner does not value or respect the other's faith. Religion is something two people need to agree on, or agree to disagree. Religion for many is the foundation of morals and values, and if principles are different, problems will arise.

Family Values

If spending time with family is important to you, then you should look for someone who values family as much as you. Oftentimes, the structure of your family will determine your future relationships and how you treat others. If you are with someone who does not respect family, you could be in for a rocky ride. And, if you are wanting to start a family of your own, this is even more important. Someone who does not value family relationships will likely not want to have one of their own. One more important note: If you enter into a relationship with someone, then you are more likely to do so with their entire family. If possible, try to get to know everyone before moving past the dating phase. When family conflicts arise, you want to know if your significant other will stand with you or against you.

Commonalities

Do opposites really attract? Perhaps initially, but if you are looking to develop a long-term healthy relationship, it is critical you share some interests! People are more likely to look for relationships with people who share similar interests, political views, goals, and more. Differences can be healthy – they can stretch you outside of your comfy place, which can be a good thing – but you should have some things that you both share that add excitement to the relationship, build your bond and keep the relationship going.

Social Behavior

If you are the exciting extrovert who is the life of every party and your partner is the inaudible introvert who refuses to go out, you may eventually grow tired of each other or find yourself single again. Why? You will end up doing a lot of things by yourself, and perhaps living a separate life, which doesn't promote a healthy relationship.

Bad Habits

Sometimes we choose to compromise on behaviors and decide that certain traits or habits that make you grind your teeth are acceptable. But if you are consciously going against something you strongly believe in, it will backfire one day and just piss you off.

A good example of going against your values in a relationship is my dating a smoker. I quit smoking and I didn't want to be with a smoker as I knew it would tempt me to start smoking again. In the beginning, I thought I could handle it, or maybe, even though he never told me he was willing to quit, get him to change his mind and butt out. He never did and I blew up at him repeatedly for doing something he had been doing when I met him. Now that I look back at this situation, I was the one at fault. I didn't want to be a smoker nor date one, so why did I date him in the first place?

People can change their habits, and often will for the sake of those they love. However, when you compromise on something that is really important to you, inevitable arguments will come. In the beginning of the relationship, it is all roses and you let things slide. But – and everyone is guilty of this – you think: "Oh I hate that, but they'll change." However, instead of just hating the habit, you end up resenting your partner.

You cannot expect people to change. Especially when they don't feel the need to change, and do not feel like they're doing anything wrong.

So if you are going to date someone who has an off-putting habit, ask them: "Do you see yourself quitting/changing someday?" If the answer is no, then do not expect to change that person. But if he or she admits to hating their own habit and says, "Yep, I've been trying to change," then sure, give the relationship a chance. Maybe a transformation is possible. But you cannot go into a relationship hoping for this. You have to actually find out before you even let them through the door.

People aren't always open to change, and you cannot enter a relationship thinking you can change who someone really is. You are guaranteed to face disappointment. So figure out if you can live with the person exactly the way they are – today. If not, then it's probably best not to go further into the relationship.

Honesty

Everyone is looking for someone who is honest. Honesty and trust go hand-in-hand and are the foundation for any relationship. Yes, we all make mistakes, but if you are attracted to someone, be sure they are truly an honest person before moving into a serious relationship. This isn't always easy to determine, I've known many men and women who had been sleeping with the enemy for many years and had no clue. It's important to be observant without being overly suspicious. Are they open with you? Do they value your opinion? Do they talk to you about everything? These are good signs of someone being trustworthy.

However, be careful not to condemn someone before they've given you a reason to. If your inner sense tells you differently, then proceed with caution – or move on before you get hurt. Remember, it is impossible to sustain a healthy relationship with someone whose behavior goes against what you believe in.

Laughing Together

I strongly believe that laughing together regularly is a sign that your relationship will be fulfilling in the long run. Laughter plays a critical role in developing a relationship, resolving conflict and creating intimacy and bonds. The playfulness that stems from laughter can also really loosen up any situation. If you can't laugh with your partner, your relationship will get boring with time. Life can be complicated and a big part of your relationship is about enjoying your life together. Find things to laugh about and enjoy the good times, or you'll just be a burden to one another and age a lot sooner than you should!

Someone with Kids

You don't like children, you never had any of your own, and you find their youthful shenanigans more annoying than entertaining. If you know you cannot deal with someone's kids, then don't pursue someone who has them. Children will never go away and will always be a priority – even though a potential marriage itself should always be the main focus.

I don't have children; that just wasn't in the cards for me. When I was younger I never met anyone with whom I could envision a bright future and, if we were not going to stay together, I didn't want to have anything tying me to that relationship. I was never one to settle for the sake of having children although I see so many people do it and that's one of the reasons why the divorce rate is so high. Dean has two children, they were in their 20s when we started dating, but honestly, if they were in their early teens when we met, that would have been a deal breaker for me. Now that they are approaching the age of having their own children, I feel kind of odd being a step grandmother when I definitely don't look or act like one. But that is much less of a deal breaker – I think! I'm not sure yet…I'll let you know in my next book. Again, know what you can live with and what you can't.

NEGOTIABLES

In this list, I've noted the most common attributes that people look for in someone else. However, these may or may not be important to you. Feel free to come up with your own list based on your likes and dislikes.

Appearance

I covered physical attraction in detail in chapter 6. Keep in mind that looks fade, so look beyond the physical and try not to make looks your number one priority. And, if everything else adds up, throw away tiny details such as he's balding or she has brown eyes instead of blue. What's most important is how you feel about yourself when you're with the other person. Don't get me wrong; you need to be attracted to the other person or the relationship simply won't work. Or, it can work if you fake attraction for the purpose of living a certain type of lifestyle that you crave and think you need.

Height

Sure, some women would love to date a Thor-like, strapping man. But if you are only 5'2", why would you need a man who is ten inches taller than you? I am not saying you should date a hobbit, but really, theme parks are less restrictive regarding minimum heights for rides than some of the women I have met. Besides, sex standing up is much better with someone closer to your own height. The height of a person should, in no way, determine your future with them. I know this for a fact.

I deviated from my norm with Dean. He is not that 6'2" bulky built man I thought I needed.

- At the end of the day, am I still attracted to him? Absolutely!
- Does he help me clean the house? Yes.
- Does he make me laugh? Yes.
- Is he the kindest guy I've ever dated? Yes.
- Does he make my life easier? Yes.
- Does he make accommodations for me? Yes.
- Does he trust me? Yes.
- Does he let me be who I want to be? Yes.
- If I gain ten pounds does he tell me I am fat? No – not yet anyway.
- Is he a gentleman who treats me like a lady? Yes.
- Do I trust that he won't leave me starving on the street? Yes.

You might even be surprised to learn that some of the world's most powerful, and influential men, are short. Iron Man, or Robert Downey Jr., is 5'8"; composer Ludwig van Beethoven, 5'3"; Mark Wahlberg, 5'8"; boxing champ Manny Pacquiano, 5'7"; producer/director Steven Spielberg, 5'7"; designer Ralph Lauren, 5'6"; J.R.R Tolkien 5'5" (Hobbit jokes not necessary); Usher, 5'8"; and inventor Isaac Newton, 5'6".

And that's just the short list (no pun intended ☺).

I'm amazed by my brother. He's only 5'7" and he often dates taller women. It's the confidence he exudes when he's around them. He loves the fact that they are taller. However, in my matchmaking practice, I notice that most men don't want to date someone taller than them. I think it makes them feel insecure.

Vegetarian-Carnivore

It would seem obvious that a vegetarian or vegan would date a savage meat eater. However, In fact, according to a match.com study of 4,000 people, only 4 percent of vegetarians or vegans surveyed said they wouldn't date a meat eater. Alternatively, 30 percent of carnivores said they would never date a veggie-loving person. The survey also shows that 66 percent of people find picky eating an unattractive quality.[4] This begs the question: Who are the picky ones, really? The easy-going vegetarians, or the carnivores who refuse to date outside of their sacred flesh-eating foodie circle?

Are food preferences really that big of a deal? Try something new; take a cooking class together and find a way to work it out!

Profession

He's a blue-collar worker and you are looking for a white-collared suit. Or, you work as a waiter at a local restaurant and you really want to date the woman who owns the restaurant. Consider my best friend, Nicole. She is married to Mike, a factory worker, and they have an amazing relationship. She couldn't possibly do better than him for a husband and I'm serious about that. She's got it made, he's classy, loyal, attractive, honest, has integrity, dotes on her, lets her sleep in while he takes care of their daughter, doesn't get upset that she doesn't cook, and the list goes on and on. If she avoided giving him a chance because of his profession, she would have missed out BIG TIME!

If this is what you really want, consider why. Do you prefer someone with an equal or higher education? Are you looking for challenging intellectual conversation or someone who will be an all-around good person? Before you judge someone based on occupation, make sure you get to know him or her first. What an individual does in their career does not necessarily reflect their personal life.

---

4   Reference:
     Match.com, Love Bites, July 2, 2012
     http://match.mediaroom.com/index.php?s=30441&item=133732

Sandy, who is in her late 30s, came to me for matchmaking help. She is a bit overweight, very successful in her career and suffers from a rare skin disorder. But, she won't settle for anyone unless he is attractive and charming, an entrepreneur who makes at least $250 thousand a year, and is so busy that he needs three cell phones to keep on top of his high-profile career. Really? Ms. Imperfect is seeking un-reality. And why would anyone want a guy with three cell phones? He would never have time to develop a relationship. I know someone who has three cell phones and he's a big-time cheater!

Neatness Counts?

Some people are neat freaks. Others could care less. Most of us are somewhere in the middle. But if this is important to you, then take note of how someone does or does not dress, or how they keep their living quarters. Keep in mind that someone who is neat will challenge your lazy side, if you are sloppy. And someone who is more laid back in this area can calm your obsessiveness for neatness. Being neat or messy does not necessarily cut into your sense of integrity, although it can burn on your last nerve. Remember, a mess can be cleaned up. But a good man or woman is hard to find.

A Spend Thrift or A Cheapskate

They say that money is the root of all evil. Actually, the wording is the love of money is the root of all evil. How does this apply to relationships? Some people love to spend money, others would rather see their bank accounts grow. In a good relationship, a couple will meet somewhere in the middle when it comes to money.

However, someone who's cheap can be a hardcore non-negotiable to a woman who loves to spend money. Dealing with someone who does not want, or can't afford to do the things you enjoy can be tricky, if not impossible.

I once dated a guy who only ever took me to the same inexpensive "restaurant" on our dates, one of those cheap, two-can-dine for $9.99 places. And despite me asking him to think outside the box to try

As you navigate through the dating scene, remember that everything you experience, good and bad, can make you a better person.

something different, it was the same old roasted chicken, fries and gravy deal. It was actually the only time we went out. He was always slacking on the couch, watching television, draining beer bottles and refused to do anything fun. He was too lazy to look for work and relied on my father to employ him. My father even loaned him his truck for six months, which he used to continue his drinking habits. After the relationship ended, I found about ten empty tall boys under the driver's seat. I asked myself a thousand times: "What was I thinking?"

It's not just that he was cheap, he was predictable and we were incompatible. I should have seen the signs at the beginning but my vision was a little clouded. I wanted a relationship so badly, I overlooked things that got in the way of actually being one. I couldn't change him (it should be known I tried) and I know he would have resented me for making him do things he had little interest in. But I can say he was a nice guy, though a deadbeat by my standards.

So how important is spending or saving to you? Realistically, this is an area you need to be able to work on with your partner.

As you navigate through the dating scene, remember that everything you experience, good and bad, can make you a better person. Take the opportunity to grow and learn something new, or something about yourself, with every date. Don't think of any date as a waste of time, even the ones that leave you speechless – and not in a good way. Think of each date as a life experience with a good story to tell. Experiences are invaluable! Learn from them, move forward and apply those life lessons to your future dates.

Let's Talk About Sex

*Y*es, we are going to jump into the sex discussion. Gone are the days when someone "saved themselves for marriage." While I'm not so sure that wasn't a bad idea, in our society sex is promoted and encouraged everywhere.

I'm not going to go into some hot and heavy, "try this position" or "this will really blow his or her mind" discussion. You can read that stuff anywhere. But I want to be frank about the role sex plays in relationships, prior to marriage. So this will be short and to the point.

A study from the National Marriage Project at the University of Virginia presents some interesting findings surrounding sex and marriage in relation to Millennials.[5]

---

5   National Marriage Project, Before "I Do." http://nationalmarriageproject.org/
    wordpress/wp-content/uploads/2014/08/NMP-BeforeIDoReport-Final.pdf
    Summary: http://nationalmarriageproject.org/wordpress/

The study found that people who had more casual sexual encounters under their belts, and more partners in general, were at greater risk for divorce. This was also true if they'd lived with partners other than the individual they married.

The research also suggests that having sex, or hooking up early on in a relationship can lead to an unsuccessful marriage later. What's more, if the relationship that led to the marriage began with a hookup, it was even more likely to be unsatisfactory. This was even true for couples that only had sex with each other before marriage.

These findings are interesting, given many feel that physical compatibility is extremely important if two people hope to have a happy marriage.

What this study suggests is that when a couple waits to have sex, it becomes more satisfactory and fulfilling in the long run. This is because the couple is fully able to ensure they're compatible on a psychological and emotional level.

In many ways, this comes as no surprise as it has been suggested that the brain is actually the most powerful sexual organ. If you're already connected to a person mentally, and physical attraction is there as well, forming an intimate relationship should be pretty easy later on.

It's also not shocking to believe that having many prior hookups can lead to an unsatisfactory marriage. It might leave you constantly comparing your partner to past encounters and wondering what else is out there. We all know that when chemistry kicks in, so does sexual arousal. I suggest establishing boundaries early in the relationship. Try not to introduce sex too quickly and watch how it is introduced. No one wants to know about your one-night stands, nor do they need to hear about the divorcee who introduced you to a world of sexual pleasure you could have never imagined! It's always best when sex comes naturally.

As I said, short and to the point. I'm not here to tell you how to run your sex life. However, given that everyone is looking for a lasting relationship at some point in their lives, it stands to reason that we should do everything possible to set ourselves up for success. But you have to define what success is in your own terms.

Chapter 9

Growing As You Date

Her name is Melissa and she keeps dating the same guy-type over and over. Guess what? She's single, again. Melissa knows what she wants and she finds it every time! Unfortunately, all she truly finds is that she's unhappy – or better yet, unsatisfied.

His name is Pete and he keeps dating the same type of woman over and over. Guess what? He's single again. Pete knows what he wants and he finds it every time! Unfortunately, all he really finds is that he's unhappy – or better yet, unsatisfied.

Do these scenarios sound familiar?

I've known women who won't date a guy because he's "too sweet." Yet these same women have their hearts broken by guys who couldn't care less about them. I've also met guys who only date "hot babes" and they end up in relationships where they feel like slaves.

Maturity is a great reality check when it comes to dating. Maturity helps you to figure out what you really need and want in a relationship. That means preferences change as we become older, because we change. Our views and values change. While dating starts off with attraction, magnetism and "goose bumps," one of those dates can become a relationship, and this is where you truly find out how compatible the two of you are. However, if you are having trouble finding someone you can get along with after the honeymoon stage, it's time to take a look at why this is happening.

Maturity helps you to figure out what you really
need and want in a relationship.

Know Your Boundaries

He's "too nice"? What is too nice? That he does not beat you up? She's too "plain Jane"? What does that mean? That she cares about you, supports you, and thinks of you first? You are missing the obvious – that he or she is really who you need in your life.

Early in my relationship with Dean, I felt he was too attentive and too sweet. He always wanted to be at my side and I felt he was smothering me. But it is in his nature to be there for me, to be present (this is why I talked about temperaments and love languages earlier). I was wrong in thinking his kindness represented a needy, weak man with no backbone. He also wasn't a pushover, nor was he someone I could dictate to and reign supreme over. Dean is incredibly confident and comfortable with who he is. I only needed to see that his behavior was well intended and that he was someone I could not let go.

So give him or her a chance. You know who I am talking about. The guy who smiles at you, or is always holding the door open for you. The girl who is naturally kind or blushes easily in your presence and you find yourself drawn to her.

You need stability in your life. What you don't need is to be with someone you can't trust, someone you suspect is cheating on you or cheating you. While some people like this kind of drama, it is not the foundation for a healthy relationship.

Here is something to consider: Do you know what your *boundaries* are in a relationship? If so, do you know how to set them? Do you know why you allow people to violate them? If not, I highly recommend the book *Boundaries in Dating: How Healthy Choices Grow Healthy Relationship* by Henry Cloud and John Townsend. Knowing your boundaries will help you identify what red flags are to you, and what are things you've previously thought were turn-offs, like that all-too-sweet man or that sensitive woman. Once you're in a relationship, most red flags are non-negotiables, and it will be nearly impossible to have a loving relationship with this person.

What Should I Be Looking For?

While you might have spent much of your dating time chasing the ever-elusive perfect person, as I mentioned in a previous chapter, he or she does not exist.

Does the perfect man make a six-figure salary, wear designer suits and shoes, has perfectly styled hair, eats at posh restaurants every night, and buys his woman gifts every week. Really?

Does the perfect woman have the face of Heidi Klum, the cooking skills of Rachel Ray, and a hot bod like Kate Upton? Let's get real.

A good man or woman has a demeanor that you're attracted to, and respects you as an equal partner. He or she doesn't blow up over every little thing; he does his best to be patient and understanding. She's willing to put up with most of your annoying habits. Yes, this person gets frustrated and upset at times. But for the most part, they know how to handle stress, disagreements, and outright arguments with maturity – not violence.

Ladies consider: How does he treat others? Is he kind? Giving? Does he have manners? Is he thoughtful and considerate? I don't mean that he buys drinks for the whole bar when he goes out or buys you a gift that wows you on your second date. I mean in the sense that he has a lot to offer and he's giving of himself to the relationship. He's willing to work on the inevitable "issues" that come up and he's willing to look at himself – not just point his finger at you.

Does he like to do the small things for you like rub your back or feet, PVR your favorite show without being asked, or bring you breakfast in bed? When someone pays attention to small gestures it really makes a big difference in the quality of the relationship.

Guys think about: How does she make you feel about yourself when you're together? Does she have your back? Can she read you so that she knows what you want? (Most women have a "sixth-sense" about their men.) Are you compatible, and I don't just mean in bed? Does she give you your space when you need it?

Here are some key points to recognize when looking for the right one:

- *Attentive:* You are the only one he or she sees when you are together. When you are out on a date, he's not checking out other women; she's not eyeing the guy at the next table. This person is fully present and engages in conversation.
- *Takes the time to get to know you:* You hardly ever hear the: "I am busy," excuse.
- *Has close family and friends:* Friends and family tell a lot about a person and their ability to handle a relationship. I always say use your gut feeling; listen to your "Spidey senses," they're usually right. Some of us ignore the signs because we want to find someone and fall in love so bad. Don't settle just because you are needy. You'll end up losing in the long run.
- *A hard worker:* A responsible man or woman who's not afraid of working is a good find. This type of person does not mind returning home after a long day at work and helping out around the house. He or she will seldom

complain or whine, but is a willing partner with domestic chores.

ⓥ *The father:* If a guy was married and has children, pay close attention to how he takes care of his children. Is he a good provider and a loving, present dad?

The Ex: Does he or she share an amicable post-marriage relationship? Now, I realize that is not the case for many ex-couples, but this does not necessarily mean the former partner is a bad person; some ex-spouses make relationships after divorce impossible. However, you are looking at their ability to take their own selfish needs out of the equation. If he or she can do that, chances are they are a good and mature person.

Things to Keep in Mind

I understand that this can be a lot to absorb. But once you make a conscious effort to make changes, you will see permanent benefits in your life! Let's now consider a few more points in helping you find the right partner.

ⓥ Find someone who complements your life and trusts who you are. Your world will change if you find a person with whom you feel secure enough to be yourself. That is, someone who accepts your sensitive side and embraces your crazy streak. Remember, relationships are meant to bring comfort and love for both of you. They are not meant to be filled with heated arguments that lead to frequent breakups. You want to be with someone who is honest and dependable, not someone who brings suspicion into your life. A lasting relationship is built on friendship, trust and integrity. Always choose a partner who will respect the foundation of trust.

ⓥ I had a habit of dating guys who were insecure and didn't accept my lifestyle. I'm an extrovert and in my line of work, I meet new people all the time, which is difficult for most guys to accept. Dean understands my personality and fully trusts me. I knew from past relationships that trust and acceptance from my partner is needed for the relationship to even stand a chance.

⚥ It's important to take a "big picture" look at any potential relationships, and look for characteristics that are fundamental. Things like empathy, integrity, honesty, kindness and generosity. Throw away the tiny details like they don't like to go club dancing, or they always eat their dinner with a spoon – no matter what's on their plate. These things don't really matter in the long term and nobody will ever meet your needs entirely. I once set up a woman of 55 with a 62-year-old man, and after the date she said that he was a really great guy. Despite this, she also said she was not interested in seeing him again because he wasn't into burning up the dance floor at bars. How many men in that age bracket are you going to find who want to go dancing at a bar, let alone burn up the floor? Not too many. It came as no surprise when she told me she was having a real difficult time trying to meet someone. Re-evaluate what is important in life and ditch things that are not.

⚥ A good relationship is more than just physical chemistry or animal-like magnetism. How do they treat you? How do they make you feel? You might feel almost "electric" when you are around someone, or even just speaking with them, but never mistake that feeling for love. Because this magnetic chemistry is so intense, it can deceive you into thinking you have found the one. I had this kind of magnetic chemistry with the guy I spoke of at the start of the book who dumped me. It wasn't until later on when I started allowing myself to heal from the breakup that I realized it was nothing more than chemistry and there was minimal compatibility. He wasn't right for me and the relationship would never have worked out in the long run.

Don't settle for someone because you're tired of seeing invitations addressed to you "and a guest" or because your biological clock is ticking and you've pushed snooze one too many times. Holding onto someone you know is not right for you can kill your spirit and leave you feeling alone. You're better off staying single until the right person comes along. Don't anchor yourself to a relationship that's destined to fail!

Holding onto someone you know is not right for you can kill your spirit and leave you feeling alone.

Section 3

Gender Specific

$\mathcal{I}$n this short section, we are going to take a good look at what men and women are looking for in a partner. But to understand the "what" it's important to understand the "why." We're going to look at why men and women are so different, so you don't go into a relationship expecting one thing, and end up getting something else. As we do this, I would like you to keep in mind my "80/20 rule." This means that what I'm about to share applies to 80 percent of one gender and 20 percent of the other. There is no such thing as "stereotypical" so feel free to find what applies to you, then you'll be much more confident in understanding what you want and need in a relationship.

Chapter 10

What A Man Wants

Ladies, Listen Up!

*W*omen, this is a must-read chapter. You may think you know what a man wants, but often that's because there are repeated phrases and sayings about men floating around in our society. But let's step away from the "canned terms" for a moment. Let's get into a man's world and see what is really going on in their hearts.

Before going into a man's world, however, I want to deal with something that is common to almost every man. Ladies, here's a question for you: Have you ever wondered why men get turned on by nudity and excitement? Yep, that's right, I want to deal with this topic right up front. Many women often see men as being "shallow" and only wanting one thing – sex, sex, and more sex. But here are a couple of things you need to know before you call all men "crass" – or worse.

First of all, men are hard-wired to be sight driven. That's right, it is part of their DNA. The reason is that men have the hormone testosterone flowing through their veins, and the more testosterone that a man has, the more driven he is by his sexual desire. That's why a man can be completely focused on a task at work or home, when suddenly a sexual thought comes into his mind and he can think of nothing else but sex.

Now this doesn't give a guy an excuse to be demanding, exploitive, controlling or manipulative. But when he's turned on because of the testosterone that's ramping up inside of him, he's going to come looking for you. That is why a good sex life is so important to a successful relationship.

Men also have a "hunter-gather" mentality. When a man is looking to date, he is actually "hunting" for his prize. When the initial attraction takes place, he then goes into "gather" mode, in which he does what he feels is necessary to win a woman's heart.

Ladies, neither of these traits mean that men have a "caveman" mentality. But if you understand what is going on inside of him, you'll have a better idea of what he's thinking and doing.

What Do Men Want?

Men are attracted to women who are sexy, and not just in a physical sense. If a woman inspires him, she's sexy. Women who are confident and comfortable with who they are, will be seen as sexy to a man. She has a lot of things going on in her life and this, to him, is exhilarating.

Let's look at some of the qualities men find attractive in women.

Strength

Are you strong? Do you stand by your beliefs? Will you be his pillar when he shows weakness or will you join him in his breakdown? When you show strength, it takes pressure off a man – he can let down his guard and he's more willing to open his heart to you. Instead of feeling like he *has* to always be there for you, he will want to be there for you.

Your strength can challenge him in good ways, and make him a better man. But if you use your strength to belittle him, you risk killing your relationship – fast! You have to know when to be the damsel in distress. It's crazy, I know, men have to hide their weakness and women have to hide their strength in order to make each other feel secure.

Spontaneity

Men love women who can go with the flow and be spontaneous. It is okay to be regimented in your work life but be more spontaneous when it comes to relationships. Men tend to be more flexible and spur-of-the-moment people, so loosen your schedule a little. (I know this because of the speed dating events I facilitate. Women tend to book further in advance and most of the men book the day before or day of.) Be adventurous. Don't let your own fears and insecurities stop you from stepping out of your comfort zone.

A Good Driver

This sounds ridiculous, but every man I have dated, made a point about my driving, whether it was good or bad. If a man gets into a car with a woman, they almost always have something to say about the driving. I think it's in their DNA. This is not a deal breaker, but being conscious of your surroundings when you drive is certainly attractive.

Be Positive

A man's role is not to make you happy; that is something you have to find in yourself. Because of their hunter-gather mentality, men tend to be more positive – they often think, "Tomorrow will be better." We all have tough days and men, especially, like to come home at night and leave the stress behind. Brighten his day with a smile and provide the happy environment that welcomes him. Think happy thoughts and have a cocktail before he gets home if you've had a bad day too. God made women the bearers of monthly misery and responsible for bringing tomorrow's humans into the world because we are capable of smiling through our pain.

A Good Cook

Many men will say that cooking skills are not just a treat; it's a special trait that can set a woman apart from all the others. The woman who takes time out of her busy day to cook for a man is a rarity today. (Yes, I realize that many men like to cook, but there is something special to a man when he's served a great meal.) And this has nothing to do with a weak woman catering to a man's need. You can be a powerful woman with a spatula in your hand! No one expects you to have the culinary skills of Martha Stewart, but there is nothing wrong with doing some traditional girly stuff, not just for him, but also for you. In a pinch, there are some very nice ready-to-heat meals at upscale supermarkets – just remember to get rid of the packaging. ☺

An old boyfriend of mine once told me that he was constantly fighting with his new girlfriend because he made the mistake of telling her what a good cook I had been and kept comparing her cooking skills to mine. I would let him wine and dine me a couple of times a week and I would pamper him with good home-cooked meals when we decided to stay in. It was my little secret weapon. Food is the way to a man's heart, and that is so true. Guys like to be taken care of and nurtured. Not in a motherly way, but in a caring way. I should have told him that telling his new girlfriend about my superior cooking skills was really stupid; and the fact that he did it constantly makes him a real jerk. But I didn't.

A Real Girl

Don't be that annoying woman who says: "I'll be ready in five minutes," and then disappears for two hours because you cannot decide what dress to wear for your trip to Walmart. High maintenance is a turn-off for most guys. Men love women who can put their hair down and be one of the guys at times, while still being the same gal who turns him on when she's all dressed up.

How long do you think you spend applying makeup each day? Sooner or later it will all come off and you'll be seen without your makeup. Guys prefer the natural, girl next-door type. Wearing too much makeup can be unattractive. Be that barefaced beauty at least once in a while and embrace your natural charm!

There is a huge difference between being the girl who has a nervous breakdown when she breaks a nail and a real girl or the girl next-door type. You can be and should be feminine or sporty when needed. The trick is feeling good about yourself. When you get over your insecurities, you'll fit into his world, knowing that you really belong.

The Compromising Conciliator

Are you the kind of woman who is argumentative and uncompromising? Men are drawn to women who are willing to find a solution and compromise, without being disgruntled over making a "sacrifice." The woman who only cares about her own opinion, wrestles a man to the ground with her mouth, will soon find she is wrestling all by herself.

Sure, men can be pig-headed and stubborn. But your ability to negotiate and compromise can calm this side of him, and he will actually start listening to you! Remember, you are wrong if you think you are right all the time.

Loving and Caring

If you are looking to bring a man to his knees, show him your nurturing side. Nurturing is something inherent to women but lacking in men, so it is a quality they respond to strongly. When you are a nurturer, he will trust that he can be real with you. You'll be his safe place. Show him how you feel, don't just tell him. A male friend of mine once told me that men are simply grown up boys. They need to be loved and cared for because it makes them feel special and valued. So take care of him. A relationship has to be give and take. It can't just be take, take, take.

Sense of Humor

Guys laugh at some of the rudest and crudest things. They can have a dry sense of humor. Guys get other guys in this area. He is not looking for you to have his sense of humor. What he is looking for is for you to have a sense of humor when things go wrong or when he does something wrong. Guys get uptight and stressed out when things aren't going as planned. But you can help him relax by not taking things so seriously; that will make him even more uptight. So look on the "bright side" or find some humor when his world isn't perfect.

Look and Smell Good

Initial physical attraction is very important to a man. If he's not attracted to you, the relationship will most likely not stand a chance. I have yet to meet a man who is not looking for a woman he finds attractive. You don't have to be a supermodel, but when you walk out that door, make sure you're the best version of you. I encourage you to enjoy taking care of yourself; dress well and feel great about how you look. Make him feel like he is the luckiest man in the room. Men love women who take pride in their appearance, and themselves overall. Do your hair, make sure your "gardens" are well manicured and, I cannot stress this enough, choose your fragrance wisely! The wrong scent, or too much of the right one can end a date before it even begins.

Scent and attraction are inseparable. How do you know you're wearing the right fragrance? People will tell you. Unfortunately, they won't necessarily tell you when you're wearing the wrong one, they'll just avoid you; but when you're wearing the right one, you will be complimented. If you're not getting compliments on your perfume, it's time to start shopping for a new one!

Unique

Don't be someone you *think* he wants you to be. Be unique by being yourself. Show your quirky side. Dare to be different. Be willing to do something audacious. Men are attracted to a fun personality, because it means they can relax and be themselves too.

Now that we've discussed characteristics that men are attracted to, let's look at a few of the things that will send them running for the hills.

Turnoffs

Do you ever wonder why the most seemingly perfect relationships fall apart? Has this ever happened to you? You find the ideal man, he meets all of your negotiables and he leaves you breathless. He's all you can think about and you can't wait for the next date.

But nothing happens.

You sit there at home, waiting for his next text or call. Nothing. Everything went so well on your first date, or so you thought. You told him to meet you at one of your favorite restaurants, you wore casual clothing so he'd see the real you, you told him about your best friend who died in a drinking and driving accident the other year, and you paid for the bill! On top of all that, you sent him a text right after you got home, asking when you could see him again. You did everything right – right? After all, you are attractive, successful and you know what you want.

Success in a relationship is not as simple as being attractive or cute. Really, you could look like a supermodel, but if he starts to back away, it is likely something about you that's making him second guess any potential relationship. Who knows, maybe talking about your friend getting killed in a drinking and driving accident was a little too heavy for a first date? Personality traits are unique to all of us, and you might not even realize you possess one of the game-killing characteristics mentioned below. And it might be one of these that makes him decide he's too busy to return your calls.

Depriving a Man of His Masculinity

With more women finding their independence and taking positions of power, unintentionally emasculating a man is becoming more and more common today. For many women, finding an equal partner – level of education, career and salary – is challenging. For some men, being with a woman who makes more money is totally taboo. You might be thinking, "What's the big deal with making more money? We have evolved as a society, right?"

Wrong.

Men are naturally inclined to be the protector and provider. That might sound ridiculous, but it is instinctual. There are studies that show most male anger stems from their failure of *feeling* like a protector, provider and lover.[6] The result of this vulnerability is depression, which materializes as anger, an emotion that temporarily allows men to feel confident. If you are a high-earning woman, make sure you respect your partner without boasting about your success.

It is okay if a woman earns a higher salary than the man she is with, but it's wrong to value money over his dignity. What I mean is you cannot be controlling and bossy – keep that behavior at work – and let your man feel he's needed.

Some men are not as sensitive and more secure, but in most cases, being with a powerful woman will cause him to feel some degree of failure and resentment.

Let him be your man. Don't always pay for everything. And respect his voice and opinion.

The Perpetual Complainer

You are turned off by constant complainers. So is he. You are not happy with your body, your career sucks and your life has no ups, only steep hills downward. Don't be the woman who always needs to be validated. Change what you can, and learn to feel good about yourself. Get active. It is amazing how exercise will change your view on life, and most importantly, will boost your self-esteem.

---

6   Psychology Today, Steven Stosny: https://www.psychologytoday.com/blog/anger-in-the-age-entitlement/201004/anger-men-and-love

Ms. Independent

Here's a truth: Men want, and need, to feel needed. Remember the guy I mentioned at the beginning of the book? The one who left me broken-hearted? I kept telling him that I did not need him and I later realized that this is the very reason he bolted. Every time we had a disagreement or an argument, I would tell him this and eventually it wore him down. He left and never looked back. If a guy threatens to leave you and you ignore him, eventually he will leave you. When you make a guy feel like you don't need him, he will likely find someone who does.

The Excessive Drinker

You like to party until you are blackout drunk, but guys don't like seeing their girls out of control like this. It is okay to be tipsy, but drink responsibly. No one wants to carry a sloppy drunk home safely. It is embarrassing, and if you act like that around the man you are with, he will always wonder what you're like when he's not there. Ladies! Keep your alcohol consumption in check! This happened to one of my guy friends and the end result was disastrous.

Rick and Kelly were going out on their third date and Kelly had reached a level of comfort where she felt she could "let loose." The two went for drinks at a local restaurant/bar and Rick ordered them a bottle of wine. Once that bottle was drained, Kelly asked for a beer. She was noticeably tipsy at this point, but he was too embarrassed to tell a 43-year-old woman to control her alcohol consumption.

As the night continued, Kelly became more drunk and got louder, slurring her words and arguing with Rick. An older man, Rick sat there in disbelief, wondering how he ever thought this girl was someone he could bring home to meet his children. Kelly had picked him up earlier in the night and she was in no condition to drive, nor was he willing to get in the car with her. He went to visit the bathroom and called a car service that would drive her home, and later return her car.

When he returned to the table, Kelly said she was hungry and put an order into the kitchen. Being a gentleman, he waited with her. He told me later that once the food came, "She was eating like a wild animal, shoving food in her mouth with her eyes half shut and her head bobbing back and forth."

When the bill arrived, it was obvious that he was picking up the $150 tab. At this point, the taxi company had been waiting outside for at least 20 minutes. Despite her despicable behavior, Rick kindly put her in the taxi and paid the driver in advance.

Once Rick returned home, he thought he was free of the Kelly drama. But at 2 am she called in a panic over her missing car.

End of relationship. That's too bad; obviously Rick is a saint!

The Sexual Virtuoso

You are an alpha woman who takes the reigns during sex, always telling him what to do and how to do it. Hear me on this, ladies. Men have fragile egos when it comes to sex. If you think you're the expert, then guide or show him in a positive way, without telling him what to do. It is one thing if he's asking, but don't be Ms. Bossy Boots in bed.

Talking Like a Trucker

Your vocabulary includes many choice/colorful expletives that you would never use around your mother.

Don't swear a lot; it is just not a feminine thing to do, and do not be the woman who uses swear words as nouns, adjectives, verbs and adverbs – yes it is possible!

It is okay to curse in appropriate context. No one can be Mother Teresa, but men typically don't like women who talk like drunken sailors.

The Never-Ending Nagger

"Clean the garage," "Don't leave your glass on the table without a coaster," "Empty the dishwasher," "Don't wear that!"

Sound familiar?

There are far more effective ways to communicate; use your secret powers of persuasion! Other than driving your man mad, incessant nagging has no real resolve. You will sound like a broken record (that is being ignored) and the continued verbal reminders will only drive a wedge between you and your partner.

Men don't like nagging. It can be a reminder of his childhood – and this is one area you don't want to sound like his mother. This is a major cause of breakups because men quickly pick up on bossy or naggy traits in a woman.

Overly Assertive

At one of my Single in the City speed dating events, Glen met Sandra and they hit it off. But when they started dating it quickly fizzled out. She showed interest but he didn't. I asked Glen why it didn't go anywhere and he said it was because she seemed like the bossy type, the girl that would start making him wear a certain type of designer underwear and pick out all his clothes. They only went out a few times.

As young girls, women are taught that being assertive and getting the best out of life is a good thing. But, is being assertive in a relationship wrong? No. Assertion is an art form. Don't be forceful and bossy. Instead, clearly communicate and don't try to "manage" the relationship. Most men steer clear of women who get serious too quickly, so in the beginning let things flourish naturally. Avoid constant texting; let him ask you out; it's okay to make plans but ask for his opinion. Men have the tendency to feel out of control when they're being chased. You don't want to reek of "neediness" so watch what you say on dates; most men seem to have a radar when it comes to bossy behavior.

The Speculator

Some women tend to speculate, whereas men say what they mean and expect women to do the same. The Speculator can look at a ten-word text and read any number of possible meanings into it. For example: "I'm running late at work, I'll just meet you there." can mean anything from: "I was talking to the hot new receptionist and time got away from me." to: "I was talking to my work buddy and he thinks I should break up with you." This can be exasperating for the man who simply meant: "I'm running late at work, so I will just meet you there!"

Always Available

Many women like to believe they are not subservient, the type that gives into everything. But when men are involved, especially in the dating stage, women have the tendency to become extremely compliant. If you are a chronic pleaser and always available, chances are you will end up with a man who will readily take advantage of you. Instead of running over at the last minute when he texts, tell him: "No, I am too busy today; how about on Thursday?" His ego might be a little bruised, but in the end, he will respect and want you far more because you have a life of your own.

If you really like a man and want to see a relationship develop, give him just a little bit – it will work in your favor. Figure out where to give him space and don't always try to be involved in what he is doing.

Chapter 11

What A Woman Is Looking For

Guys, Pay Attention!

*I*n 2003, a movie came out titled "What a Girl Wants" starring Amanda Bynes. In 2009, Christina Aguilera sang a hit song with the same title. (But don't confuse this with the movie "What Women Want" staring Mel Gibson because we all know he doesn't know a thing about what women want.)

Guys, "what a girl wants" is a popular theme in a woman's world. You might think you know what a woman wants but from my experience, there are a lot of you out there that do not! Remember, women don't think like you do. Here are some traits that will draw the heart of a woman to you, so get your study hat on.

To start with, a confident man is a turn-on to any woman. This guy knows what he wants and isn't afraid to go after it. He can make decisions, and doesn't defer everything to her. Now there's a difference between asking for her input and asking her to decide, and a self-assured man understands this. If you don't appear comfortable in your own skin, then you really need to take a look at where your fears and insecurities come from. The first step towards developing confidence is understanding yourself, and getting some help. I'll give you some self-confidence booster tips later on in the book, but for now, here are some other female heart-grabbers.

Intelligence

Sapiosexual: One who is attracted to intelligence or the human mind.

Women love men who are intellectually mature. This doesn't mean flashing your Harvard degree in her face or espousing words that are meant for a PH.D. seminar, but more so a general knowledge of what's happening in the world around you. Know a little about everything, and know how to talk about subjects *without* getting heated. It's a great way to keep a woman interested and the conversation going!

The Protector

A woman adores a man who wants to protect her. This man makes her feel safe and secure, both physically and in their relationship. The safer a woman feels with you, the more she'll respect you and want to be around you.

Someone Challenging

Women are turned off and scared off by men who pay too much attention to them, this is where you need to tone down your "hunter-gatherer" mentality. Always go easy, start slow, and don't make yourself available all the time. Show her that you have other things going on in your life; that is attractive. What is not attractive is a man who is excessively clingy.

Attentiveness

"Huh?" you say. Am I contradicting myself? No, I'm not. If you smother her with attention when you start dating, you'll set yourself up for a pattern that you can't possibly keep. But think about this: Women are highly sentimental and love to know someone is thinking fondly of them. Here's the key: Pay attention to her *actions* and things she *says*. This is a lot easier than you might think. Notice the little things, like if she gets her hair cut be sure to pay a respectful comment. Guys, here's a hint: Keep a list of things she likes, says, or does. When the right time comes, you'll be able to say the right thing, slip her a "thinking of you card" or send her a "thinking of you" text that lets her know you really care.

Trust

We women want to trust our men – and we want them to trust us. I'm talking about a man who isn't jealous and isn't worried when his woman goes out with her girlfriends – you know the suspicious FBI type that asks you a gazillion questions to try and catch you in a lie or frequently checks the condom box to see if there are any missing. That's annoying!

Generosity

Women love a man who is generous. But be careful of this at the start of a relationship. A small gift or card is a great way to capture her heart. But if you come on too strong with gifts and trips and other things, she'll wonder what you're up to. She may even feel she has to reciprocate, and she may not be ready for that. So don't go out of your way to break your bank and win her over. Remember, generosity is best in small doses when a relationship is just starting.

A Great Lover

Have you heard of the three-date rule? Many women tell each other, "Never sleep with someone until at least the third date." You may be hot to trot the first time you both go out, but show her respect – and some self-restraint. If the night leads to an overnight, then it will be natural for both of you.

When you're between the sheets, a woman becomes instantly addicted to a skillful lover who can make her feel good and teach her new ways of feeling incredible. Boys, perfect your moves! Great advice, right?

Here's the problem. You know what turns you on, but do you have any idea what "rocks her world"? Many guys don't. "Wham, bam, thank you ma'am," is a common thought of a guy, but what about her needs? Hear me out: If you don't have a clue about a woman's body, there are great books available. We aren't talking about porn material and magazines. Instead, let your fingers do the walking through an online bookstore and find a good book on love-making. And when the time is right, you'll both be glad you did.

Romance

Guys, sex isn't romance, at least most of the time. Romance for a woman comes in different forms, and you'll be doing you both a favor if you read, study, and memorize the prior section of *The Five Love Languages*. Even if a woman denies being the romantic type, trust me she is. Whether wining and dining means a five-star restaurant or a burger and fries, women love to be taken out for a meal. However, if she is making you dinner, don't ever show up to her place without something in hand. Here's a tip: If you really want to win her heart, forgo a day of sports watching with your friends.

Take the Lead

With more and more women being in management positions in their careers today, women like to take a more compliant role in their personal lives. Many women are attracted to decisive men who take the initiative and make things happen. So set yourself some goals and chase them with passion. Don't mistake this for permission to be bossy or aggressive. Women are not looking to be controlled or ordered around.

Be a Gentleman

Guys, be classy! Women love men who are courteous and do things like open doors, or pull out a seat. Extra points if you are a man who has an understanding of fine wine and fashion – this does not mean you have to discuss the latest trends on the catwalk – but a touch of class can go a long way.

Melanie met Drew, a funeral director, online. For their first date, Drew picked her up and took her to dinner. Drew was just as she had hoped – tall and attractive.

On their way to the restaurant, she noticed a bottle of bleach in his back seat. Curiosity prevailed and she asked why it was there. Drew explained that sometimes his car overheats and he'd use what was in the bottle to cool off the radiator.

Dinner was a success but the drive home proved … different. The car started to overheat and steam billowed from the hood. Drew pulled into a parking of a funeral home he was once employed, and said he was going to fill the bottle of bleach.

He opened the hood of the car, and she could see his exposed privates, which were at eye level (he was 6'3") between the gap. He started peeing in the bottle! Shocked, she rolled down the window and suggested he go inside, somewhere more private, to relieve himself. He soon came back out, holding the bottle, and continued filling the radiator with the liquid.

However, he wasn't quite finished (perhaps Melanie had interrupted his peeing in a bottle moment), because Drew then said he still had to go to the bathroom. And that's just what he did – at the back of the building. Apparently urinating in public did not bother him, nor did he care about washing his hands.

The message in that bottle was delivered loud and clear.

Don't be a Neanderthal, especially on a first date!

A Funny Guy

I understand that not everyone is funny. If you are one of these people who lacks a sense of humor, don't try be the funny guy; this can backfire. At the same time, don't be one of those stiffs who never laughs or smiles. Be the man who can see the humor in life, and show your easy-going side.

Live a Little

Women like men who can share adventures and have some fun. Instead of taking them to your local pub on a date, try something new. Try an activity-based date like go-carting or visiting a museum. Better yet, find something she is interested in. A good friend of mine started dating a woman he was extremely smitten with. He found out she used to play the violin, second chair, in high school and college. He also took note of her favorite music conductor. When her favorite orchestra came to their city, he arranged for his lady to go back stage and meet the violinists and the conductor. Needless to say, this happy couple is still together years later.

The Real World Of Dating

At this point in the book, you should be feeling pretty confident. You know a lot more about yourself, about who to look for, and you've got a solid understanding of what Mr. or Ms. Right is looking for as well. Now we are going to enter the real world of dating.

Our electronic age begs singles to put their best selves out there, and a dating profile is a great place to start. However, I've read some really boring and some downright terrible profiles. That's not to say the person is boring or terrible; they simply don't know what to write about themselves. The truth is we all have that problem. It's easy to talk about ourselves, but writing? Highlight your best qualities in your profile. Define a specific type of man/woman you are looking for and create a profile that will appeal to that group. Message people and have conversations. Be open-minded and give people a chance.

Let's Get Going

"Why am I not meeting anyone?"

I've heard that question many times in my matchmaking business. The truth is there is no one way to meet people, and there is no one thing you should be doing. And maybe that's the point. You are doing the same thing over and over. You know what they say about the definition of insanity: It's doing the same thing over and over and expecting different results.

In this chapter, I'm going to offer you suggestions that will help you think outside of your boxed-in habits. Don't leave your love life to chance! You've got to get out there and go find it.

These days, it is less likely that someone will sweep you off your feet. Don't expect he will miraculously show up at your door; the only people who do that are kids peddling confection or those sneaky sales reps trying to catch you off guard. And don't expect her to just walk into your local hangout looking for Mr. Right. Go look for the person who will set your heart a flutter. If you are the type who immediately returns home after work, without seeing friends or participating in some kind of activity, then check out your local "what's happening" website. If you're too timid to go to an event by yourself, then invite a friend. Just don't lean on him or her to make the initial contact, if you spot a cute guy or gal. *You* need to make the first move, or your friend may end up being the one who gets lucky. I am talking about initiating conversation, not just spouting off a pick up line. Take a chance! The only thing you have to lose is the chance to lose yourself in love.

Ladies First

Ladies, stop thinking that he should approach you and not vice versa. Those days are over! It is a two-way street. A misconception that women have is that men don't like it when women approach them. This is not true. When I was single, and had my eye on a guy, I'd think of a way to strike up a conversation. I might have offered a compliment, asked for directions, or made a reference to my surroundings, or just flat out handed him my number. Ballsy? Yes! But it worked a lot of times. Most men find it flattering when women approach them; it usually catches them off guard.

In fact, Single in the City surveyed 100 single men and asked if they approved of women making the first move. 98 percent said "yes or why not," and 25 percent preferred taking the lead.

Get in his way and give him a reason to strike up
a conversation with you.

Granted, some women are only attracted to men who initiate. But if you are like that, you may be waiting a long time to find your dream partner. There are various reasons why a man won't approach a woman he is interested in. He may be shy, nervous, or afraid of rejection. He may not be picking up on your signals, or perhaps hasn't noticed you. He may also be thinking you have a boyfriend, or that you're out of his league and you get hit on too much. Give him a reason to get to know you.

One guy told me that he had his eye on a lady at a local dance club and was debating the best way to approach her. A minute later, she came strolling past him and "bumped" into him, then kept walking to the ladies room. He was waiting for her when she came out, and their conversation soon led to their first date. Get in his way and give him a reason to strike up a conversation with you. Ladies, feel free to use any of the confidence booster tips and approaching techniques that I am about to unveil in Guy Talk; they can also apply to you.

Guy Talk

Guys, please listen to what I'm about to say and know that I have your best interests at heart.

There are still countless women who won't approach a man, but are waiting for him to make the first move. In my matchmaking services, I hear women often complain about not getting approached, and it really bothers them. I ask every new male matchmaking client whether or not they approach women, and I would say that 7 out of 10 say no! I know, it can be scary, but you need to do what you have to do to gain the confidence to go after what you want, otherwise you're wallpaper. Women can be scary, but only as scary as you allow them to be. I know that many men are afraid of "feminazis," and, I'm not going to lie, they do exist. But generally, women just want equal pay for equal work, and the right to choose what they do with their own bodies – when it comes to dating, most would prefer you take the lead.

You remember that cute woman you saw at the coffee shop. You know, the one with gorgeous hair and dazzling smile. She's the one who glanced over at you, but shyly turned her head away when you refused to return the welcoming glance? That girl!

Men, I want to set the record straight. Even if this is the 21st century, I cannot stress enough how important is to surrender to old-fashioned dating habits and use your primal male tendencies. Chivalry is not dead. It may be on life support, but women everywhere are hoping for a miraculous recovery. Everyone has a special niche, and you have to figure out what yours is and use it. So go ahead and ask a woman out!

Guys, *every* woman is attracted to a confident man. Self-confidence is the belief in your own abilities and power to follow through on your plans.

How you regard yourself has a huge impact on how others view you. The more self-assured you are, the more likely you are to succeed. The more fearless you are, the easier it will be for you to approach women. For some, fearlessness may come easy, but others have to work hard at it. As promised, here are some self-confidence booster tips to improve your personal outlook:

- □ **Dress properly.** Women love a guy with a sense of style. You don't have to be GQ, but whatever you do, make sure your clothes fit your body properly. There are date coaches and personal shoppers in your area who will take you shopping and/or you can go to a popular clothing store and ask for a salesperson who will assist you and give you an objective opinion. Easy, done! Groom and look good when you go out that door. And don't forget to stop by your favorite department store and let the ladies behind the counter find a fitting scent for you that will melt her heart. A man that smells good can be very inviting. Also, if you're a size 32 waist, don't wear a size 36! If you're a medium don't wear an extra-large because it's cozy. Wear the cozy clothing when you're at home alone, not on a date, at work or just out and about.
- □ **Maintain good posture.** Sit up straight, just like your mother used to tell you.
- □ **Exercise regularly.** Working out releases endorphins, which makes you feel good and look good, and a woman loves to hear that her guy goes to the gym or participates in sports regularly.
- □ **Attend speed dating events.** You could consider these as "dating practice," and the more you date, the easier it gets.

☐ **Use positive affirmations.** Affirmations are short, powerful statements that you acknowledge to be true. They can be extremely persuasive tools in helping to get your statement to stick in your head. You know that saying, "Be careful what you think and say because it may come true."

Here are five positive affirmations that can change your life forever. Make sure to repeat these affirmations on a daily basis so they become routine to the point where your brain starts to absorb them, and they form the thoughts that create your reality:

I.   I love and accept myself deeply and completely.
II. I love challenges, they bring out the best in me.
III. Nothing is impossible and life is great.
IV. I have a powerful belief in myself.
V.   I am a success in all that I do.

Guys, *every* woman is attracted to a confident man.
Self-confidence is the belief in your own abilities
and power to follow through on your plans.

Once you start building up your confidence and gain the nerve to approach women regularly, you will get better and approaching will become second nature. You'll be a pro!

Approaching someone you're attracted to takes some courage – I understand that; you just have to keep practicing over and over again and eventually someone will respond.

Eye contact is a great indicator to know if someone is interested in you. You can approach a woman when you're being somewhat invited or when it's unexpected. A simple glance, a smile, then look away. No creepy stares; you just want her to know that she's been noticed. That initial eye contact may happen a few times before you strike up the nerve to have a conversation.

Take this tip from a friend of mine: You've got nothing to lose! If he saw an attractive woman at a store or the mall, he would keep her within eyesight. He would check her left hand to make sure she wasn't wearing a wedding ring. When he had the chance, he would politely approach and start-up a conversation based on something going on in his surroundings.

When you're approaching a woman, think of something interesting that will help strike up a conversation. You can use what's happening around you to draw her into a conversation or you can ask her about something common to the immediate space.

- *Coffee Shop Example*: "Hi there! I'm wondering if you've tried the Pumpkin Spice Latte? Or maybe you can recommend a different drink?
- *Mall Example*: Hi there! I just bought this jacket but I'm not too sure about it and wanted a woman's advice. Do you like the jacket? You can be honest.

  - *Department Store Example:* "Hi, sorry to intrude, but can I ask you a question? I have to get a gift for a work colleague and I'm completely stumped, I don't know what's considered appropriate anymore, do you think (offer up a suggestion, i.e., perfume) is acceptable?"
  - *Grocery Store Example*: "Excuse me, I am wondering if you can help me pick out a ripe avocado? I'm trying to make guacamole for the first time, but have no idea when an avocado is perfect for the picking. Do you have a great recipe for guacamole?"
  - *On the Street Example*: Excuse me, I'm new to this area. Do you know where _____ is? It looks like you're going that way; would you mind if I walked with you?"

Engaging conversation will always help you determine if there is any level of compatibility or chemistry. Remember, you are not asking her to marry you! You are looking to find out if you are both interested in meeting somewhere or going on a casual date. And always be observant. If she seems uninterested, and is playing on her phone or her eyes are wandering in every direction to avoid meeting your eyes, then leave her alone. Women will give you signs they are not interested, and they won't require a decoder ring if you are paying attention.

If, however, she takes the time to engage you in conversation, and responds by asking you questions, then you may be on to something. But don't overstay your welcome. Have a light conversation, then excuse yourself. If there's an opportunity, tell her you would like to see her again, and ask for her number or give her yours. You can also ask for her email instead of a phone number. Some women feel more comfortable giving out an email as its less forward and low-risk.

Look Around

Whether you're a guy or a gal, I'd like to ask you: How many people do you meet in a week? By "meet," I mean how many do you interact with socially through eye contact and a conversation? If you are meeting one individual a week, think about how long it will take you to find someone you're interested in. And if you are not meeting at least one person each week, then you can't say, "Why doesn't anyone want to date me?"

In order to meet the right somebody, you need to meet a lot of people, and not just accept the first one who comes along. Set a goal to meet at least four people a week, which amounts to 208 potential dates each year. Out of all those people, there may only be forty-fifty that you would actually want to date. And there may only be twenty that you would consider seeing again. But of that twenty, you may find five that have long-term potential – and those are good odds in your favor. It really is a numbers game.

What do you do if you don't know how to meet others? What I mean is, you get tongue-tied and jittery at the thought of taking that first step. If you have a friend of the opposite sex, then talk to him or her. Better yet, practice your approach. Rehearsal is a great way to build confidence. Also, hang out with a group of co-workers and actually participate in the conversation, not just listen to what others are saying. The more comfortable you are with approaching people, and engaging them in conversation, the less likely you will be intimidated when speaking with that individual you've been eyeing. You'll feel confident that you can start a casual conversation.

Here are some examples of making conversation in your daily routine.

- If you go to the gym, talk to at least two people before you leave. Make observations, ask questions and make comments.
- Practice giving compliments. You could be standing in line somewhere and someone next to you could be wearing something that flatters them. You'd be surprised on how interactive people can get when you pay them a compliment. Clothing, shoes, and glasses are three great things to focus on.
- If you go out for lunch or dinner with friends or coworkers, spark up a conversation with the wait staff. They are generally very friendly and willing to interact.
- Talk to the checkout clerk at the grocery store. He or she can always use a little conversation or chuckle to break up the monotony of their job.

If you are serious about meeting someone then put yourself in the path of luck, start talking and try something new!

Don't procrastinate when it comes to finding love, unless you're really *not ready* to meet someone. But if you are, put yourself out there, take action and open yourself up to possibilities.

If you set out to find love, you *will* find it. Create rituals for yourself, set goals. If you are serious about meeting someone then put yourself in the path of luck, start talking and try something new!

Chapter 13

Online Dating

Remember that feeling you'd get in your stomach, when you'd lock eyes with that cute one across a crowded room? Then remember how your heart leaped at the sound of their voice the first time the two of you went out?

Fast forward twenty years. In our society, web searches, texting and more have replaced much of the initial one-on-one contact. For online dating, the "refine search" function has become your best friend:

- Height
- Age
- Ethnicity
- Education
- Body Type
- Proximity

For women, it's like shopping for shoes. For men, it's like checking out a new car. Only better.

Some might think online dating only nurtures commercial happiness and promotes sexual promiscuity. I disagree. Online dating sites offer a convenient community for people who are serious about meeting others with specific qualities and traits. The dating pool has become infinite, unrestricted by geography or by your local watering hole.

The concept of this type of dating is not a new one. In fact, personal dating/matchmaking services date back as far as the 1700s. Back then, a "matrimonial service" was offered; there was no dating, only arranged marriages and/or courtships. These matrimonial agencies were the equivalent of today's matchmaking services. Individuals would pay agents to print ads for people looking for a spouse. After all, being single after 21 was shameful.

Today, "sight unseen" kind of dating has evolved dramatically, from personal ads to TV ads to chat rooms to official Internet dating. It all started with the inception of Match.com in 1995. Maybe some of you have heard of Gary Kremen, CEO and founder of Match.com. In his first major media interview, Kremen made the bold declaration: "Match.com will bring more love to the planet than anything since Jesus Christ."[7] Naturally his publicist was mortified. But the perfect marriage of his innovation, eccentricity, and confidence catapulted Match.com into one of the world's top dating sites. Today Match.com is operated by IAC Interactive (IAC Personals, that also runs OkCupid. com, Chemistry.com, Plenty of Fish and Tinder). The online dating industry as a whole is valued at almost $2.5 billion.

Over the past two decades, the increasing popularity of online dating has completely overturned traditional dating rules. And determining how to present yourself, with the numerous algorithms used to find your perfect match, has become more of a science than

---

7   Business Insider: http://www.businessinsider.com/how-matchcom-was-founded-by-gary-kremen-2015-7

a form of art. Online dating has been proven to expand your social circles. Through the click of a button or the swipe of a screen, you have the potential to meet countless new people. But even though the opportunity is superlative, online dating can be a mind-boggling and frustrating experience. You may experience the "paradox of choice."

For those who have not heard about this phenomenon, Psychologist, Barry Schwartz launched this concept in a 2005 Ted Talk. The paradox of choice was created as a result of western industrial societies' pursuit to maximize individual freedom. Embedded in this pursuit, is the belief that the way to maximize freedom is through more choice and through more choice, is more freedom. Choice essentially means freedom! Schwartz also talked about the negative effects of too much choice as a result of this pursuit for freedom. He states that too many choices can result in:

1. *Paralysis*. People find it difficult to choose. As a result, they become overwhelmed and, therefore, can't or don't end up making a choice.

2. *Low satisfaction and escalation of expectations*. Even if you're able to overcome the paralysis of choice, you may end up less satisfied. The more options you have, the easier it is to think you could have made a choice that was even better. Even when a choice is made, it can create an escalation of expectations, as well as thoughts such as, "Could I have done even better?" The anticipated regret can leave you with feelings of being less satisfied.

Having said this, don't feel disheartened. This chapter will help you navigate the online dating scene. If online dating is new to you, you were in a long-term relationship and are now ready to start dating, or if you want to beef up your profile, here is a guide, to help you in your quest to find "*the one*." I can help you find success in the online dating world by representing the best possible version of yourself.

Stand Out

Welcome to online dating! One of the first things you'll need to do is write a strong dating profile. But if you're like most people, you wonder what to say and how to say it. The right words will either attract or turn people away from your page. You want to be honest and sincere, but not come across as a salesperson. Nor do you want to be the popular Mexican artist Frida Kahlo, who is internationally known for her masterpiece – a self-portrait of a woman with what seems to be facial hair.

Treat your online dating profile like you would your resume, if you were looking for a job. Put your best foot forward and stand out from the rest. Be appealing but *do not lie* in your write up.

You're now ready to create your profile. With the material we have previously covered, you should have a good idea of who you are and what you are looking for in a date/relationship. You should also have at least a general idea of who you are looking for. Here are some profile tips that will help you stand out:

- Look your best. Sure you want to wear comfy clothing but don't be sloppy. Guys, don't post a picture wearing a scruffy tee-shirt and baggy jeans; that's never a good look. And ladies, if you're going for "sexy," there's a fine line between sexy and looking like you just slid off a stripper pole.
- Ladies, a bit of skin is good, but leave the rest to the imagination so you can attract the right kind of guys. They say women who show cleavage are messaged more but then who's messaging them? Sex anybody?
- Be honest with whom and about what you are looking for.
- Have patience.
- Create a well thought out profile.
- Make a list of your hobbies that make you unique and different; list things that are uncommon.
- Sure you need to say your must-haves and no-no's. But you don't want to overwhelm your dating pool with such particular information. Instead, use these as a guide to help others find you.

Create a Catchy Username

Your username can either make or break your online dating world. While not all sites require one – some allow you to use your real name – many still require you create something that identifies who you are.

This is how people recognize you so it should be well thought out. It could be a word that best describes your personality, something you like to do or an activity you enjoy.

Examples:

- *FunLovingSmartyPants*
- *LuvWarmHugs*

ⓦ *MumsLoveMe*
ⓦ *HandsomeSailor*
ⓦ *FunnyChefGirl*

Whatever username you choose, the goal is to get an individual's attention quickly. Between a great picture, a fun or clever name and a well thought out headline, you've greatly increased your chances of grabbing someone's attention. Speaking of headlines, here are some catchy examples:

ⓦ Full of life and ambition seeks the same.
ⓦ Once in her life, a woman is entitled to fall madly in love with a complete gentleman.
ⓦ Health, fitness and dancing shoes.

Writing Your Profile

Now that you've completed the preliminaries, it is time to write your profile. This might seem like a daunting activity, but if you do it correctly, you will be able to attract the right kind of attention.

When you are writing your profile, keep it short and sweet. People have the attention span of a goldfish. In fact, studies show the attention span of a human has dropped from 12 seconds in the year 2000 to only eight seconds today. Goldfish if you are wondering, apparently have an attention span of at least nine seconds.[8] Scary? So don't write a novel. These days, a long profile will seem like an eternal novel.

The best online dating profile focuses on what makes you unique. Try looking at other profiles in your demographic; what could you highlight on your profile that no one else is talking about? Stating that you like to go to the gym, hanging out with friends and love your family, is pretty generic and common. Instead, succinctly state why you go to the gym,

---

8   Microsoft Study, summarized in Time magazine; Now you Have a Shorter Attention Span than a Goldfish, May 14 2015
     http://time.com/3858309/attention-spans-goldfish/

why you love your family, and what makes your friends special. Have you travelled anywhere recently that you loved? Is there something that you can do that no one would ever guess i.e. hobby, work related? Do you have a funny or cute nickname? Think about adding information that will highlight your personality, humor and true interests.

Ultimately, you want to use descriptive words that reflect your true personality. The best dating profiles are the ones that can capture their readers with a few short sentences. If you run into difficulties, ask a friend how they would describe you and have them help you write up a mock profile.

Be positive and as honest as possible about who and what you are looking for. Imagine you're talking to your ideal partner. What would you say? What makes you a great choice for him or her? Everyone thinks they're funny, laid back, adventurous and so on. If you are those things, find a unique way to express those characteristics.

You love your family and friends?

When someone is close to their family and friends, it tells others they are a stable person. However, don't make this the focus of your profile. Instead, express your value and interests. People want to know about you, not your relatives. You might write: "I love going to the movies on Friday nights with my close friends."

Be interesting!

"I like this I like that, I don't like this and I don't like that. I especially don't like…" An endless list of your likes and dislikes are sure to turn people off. Those who read your profile want to know what sets you apart: An avid sports activity or unique job; are you an outdoors or indoors person and why; concerts, cottaging. For instance, "I love swimming at the cottage, it is my favorite thing to do" tells a lot about you in a few words.

Everyone is a comedian

Think you are funny? Prove it! Write down something funny so your readers can chuckle. But if you're not the funny type, don't say that you are; this will come out on your first date, and that won't be anything to laugh at either.

Use descriptive language

Focus on the important points about you; maybe five adjectives that best describe who you are. What makes you special and unique? Develop a short description around each adjective. Here are some words that conjure up good vibrations: *Adorable, courageous, a go-getter, approachable, compassionate, clever, easygoing, social, passionate, playful, thoughtful, creative, energetic, intelligent and open-minded.* However, be careful with the words you choose. You might end up targeting people who resonate with those words – *shy, introverted, quiet, crazy or homebody* – and eliminating options, like extroverted people who are completely sane, outgoing and occasionally enjoy a night out on the town.

Provide examples

Instead of just saying you are into travel, write: "Last year I travelled a lot, and my favorite place was Bangkok. I loved the experience it offered." This also shows you have an adventurous side. Examples are a great way to let someone into your life. But, err on the side of caution and don't share too much information. Your goal is to entice interest, without leaving people shaking their heads, thinking: "TMI!"

No clichés

Avoid clichés, things like: "*I like candlelight dinners,*" or "*Walks along the beach.*" What beach? Where? "*I'm looking for my better half.*" "*Are you my partner in crime?*" (Thank you, but I stay on the right side of the law). "*I hate people that lie,*" (really? I thought everyone loved liars!) "*I'm looking for my prince charming.*" "*My friends and family are important to me.*" (Aren't they important to everyone?)

Here is one of my pet peeves: "*I work hard and play hard.*" What does that mean? You pound cement all day, then go home to down a case of beer? Guys, I can assure you: That cliché is a turn off to women. And women, please don't write: "*Tired of drama and games.*"

What you're really telling guys is you're simply tired of relationships. And how about these: "I love to have fun." "*I love to laugh,*" "*I like to be adventurous.*" That's all just boring stuff.

Spell Check

There is nothing worse than reading something like: I am a vry xcting pple and u should connet w/me. What? *Please,* use proper spelling and grammar. You can always write your profile out in a Word document, which will help fix grammar and spelling, then cut and paste. You have no excuse for errors in your profile!

Show Some Humility

Don't brag about your looks or how much attention other people give you. It's okay to say you're handsome or attractive, but don't rant about your looks. Doing so will make others think you are high maintenance and full of yourself. The truth is that people who speak highly of themselves are usually insecure and need reassurance.

Be Real

How would you feel if you liked someone's picture, but when you met them in person, you found out that picture was taken ten years earlier. Be true to who you are; don't pretend to be someone else and post a recent picture, within the last six months to a year. Dishonesty and first date disappointment are the quickest ways to ensure you stay single.

Your CTA

Last, but not least, end your profile with a sentence that will entice someone to contact you, or let you know they are interested. This is your call to action! For example, if you are into golf, say: "I recently won a golf tournament at the Golf on the Greens challenge, and I'd like to win you over too. If you are looking for someone to hit some golf balls with, let's meet up at the driving range!"

Sample Profile

Username: *EntreprenuerLadyLove*
Headline: *Adorable chef looking to try out her new cookbook!*
Hi There,

I am Laura! I am a passionate, life-loving chef and entrepreneur. One of my favorite things to do is to experiment in the kitchen with different recipes and taste pallets. Cooking up savory meals for my friends and family is the ultimate currency for me. Not to brag or anything, but I am known for my famous homemade, Italian prosciutto thin crust pizza! What is your favorite meal? I am always open to new taste testers ☺.

In my downtime, my dog Max and I love to explore new trails. I am convinced that aside from humans, dogs are the most loving creatures on the planet – who agrees with me? If you know of any cool hiking trails that are dog friendly, Max and I would love to hear from you! When I am not cooking up a storm or out with Max, I enjoy swimming in my pool and nights out, finding new, local and live music venues.

I pride myself on making the most of every situation I encounter. I'm told I am witty, and I love to make people laugh. I'm also extremely loyal to those I love.

I am looking for a man who is ready for a relationship with an attractive, successful woman. A man who likes his nights out exploring the city, just as much as staying home snuggling on the couch with me.

Now that you know a little bit about me, I look forward to learning more about you!

Laura

If you are not a good writer, hire an expert to write your profile or have your friends help you out – and friends might also have a better perception of who you are, and can give you advice on pictures as well. Online dating is an accepted norm and you don't have to be secretive. When I launched Single in the City more than fifteen years ago, it was kind of taboo. At that time, no one wanted to admit they had an online profile and many profiles were hidden for anonymity.

Today, profiles are usually hidden due to infidelity so beware of hidden profiles!

And *always* include a photo: People who upload a photo get more attention than those who do not.

A few points to remember:

- Spelling errors (teh, u, cuz, dont or b4) in a profile result in a -13 percent interest.
- Full body photos boost both sexes by a staggering +203 percent.
- Users who mention "book," "write" or "read" in their profiles have a +21 percent lift.
- +21 percent gain when "jogging," "running," "weights" or "yoga" are used.
- Men who mention drinks, dinner or lunch in first message: -35 percent response.
- Women who mention drinks, dinner or lunch in first message: +73 percent response.
- Men get 8 percent fewer messages if they post selfies.
- Talking about kids and exes gets men more messages but women fewer.

Honesty, patience and a well thought out profile are what you need to begin your journey towards finding true love. Always keep these three things in mind when constructing your user profile:

1. Be short, sweet and to the point.
2. Clearly state who are you, what you are looking for and why should they pick you.
3. How can you design a profile that will make you stand out from everyone else's profile.

Online Photos

Marnie is 5'2" and a highly successful businesswoman, looking for someone equally successful and attractive. She takes care of herself and knows what she wants. Marnie was drawn to Derek's profile. This was her first online adventure so she had not yet been sullied by the online masses. She hadn't thought to interrogate him; she trusted him as honest.

Derek seemed to fit her needs. The only photo he had displayed was a headshot, and he quite willingly sent her more pictures – all of his head.

Over the next two weeks, the pair texted one another and started to develop a relationship. Then they planned to meet.

Here is Marnie's story:

It was my first online date ever and it turned out to be with a "little person." We spoke for over two weeks via text, and over the phone before meeting. He only had a headshot on his profile and all the other pictures he forwarded were the same. I never thought about asking for his height because I figured unless you were a 10-year-old boy, you would probably be taller than my 5'2" stature.

We met at a Starbucks and I was shocked! Of course the only seats available were the damn bar stools! I instantly broke out into a sweat thinking I would need to lift him up or give him a boost. The sad thing is that I really connected with him over the phone and over text. He didn't once mention his height. I need a man who cannot see his reflection in my belt buckle while standing up.

Following her sobering first date, Marnie is now far more suspicious with her online dates. She has since been on many of dates and is still hopeful that she will find the right one.

Moral of the story? Photos can be deceiving! As a matchmaker, and once upon a time serial online dater, I've seen countless people look much better in person than in pictures and vice versa. If you are going to take online dating seriously, you have to realize that people are three-dimensional. Not two-dimensional like a photo. A photo will tell you very little about an individual and they can easily be touched up.

You can't see someone's personality through pictures and you'll never know what kind of chemistry you share. People can be made to look gorgeous in photos, but when you see him or her in real life, the reality might cause you to choke. And maybe that person is not so driven by appearance, he or she displays photos that don't highlight their best angles. The worst kept secret, of course, is photo editing software. Be careful. If there's an element you didn't notice before posting, understand that the World Wide Web will. There are many websites devoted to "selfie fails" and the comment section is brutal. Don't be one of them, you're looking for a date, not auditioning for a spot on Ripley's Believe it or Not: Freaks of Nature Edition.

Let's be realistic. How many people do you meet, or do you see out there, who are exactly what you are looking for? Hardly any. So if everyone based their search on looks, it would be like trying to find a straight guy in a gay bar.

Yes, take the person's picture into consideration, but don't just base your yes or no solely on that image. If you look at it and cringe, move on. But if there's something there, what have you got to lose? Especially if you read a profile that matches what you are looking for, or meets some of your expectations. If something he or she says sparks your interest, then explore further.

If you are going to take the time to start an online dating profile, it is in your best interest to post a few good pictures of yourself. As humans, we are inherently judgmental. It is only natural for us to form an opinion based on experiences or learned preferences. A first impression is drawn from your photos, instead of your demeanor, body language or how you are dressed, so make sure your photo is a home run!

Action Shots

Pictures should be of you and not scenery from places you have travelled. It is okay to be in photos where you are taking part in a hobby or from recent vacations because active photos can be a good conversation starter. But don't be that teeny, weenie object that's disappearing in the background. Yes I know the Swiss Alps are gorgeous, but you are not trying to sell a vacation to Switzerland. It is okay if you are doing an activity where someone can actually see what you look like in action, because that's a different form of you. Just remember that you're showcasing yourself so your picture must feature you.

If you like hiking, show a picture of you on a trail. If you spend a lot of time at a cottage, consider posting one of you outdoors to illustrate your passion. It is also okay to post a photo of you out on the town, if you are one of those club-hopping, party-going types. But, keep in mind photos that show your party animal side might attract the wrong kind of person. If, however, you are looking for someone who will embrace and complement your wildly unpredictable side, then choose photos that best illustrate the true you. Just make sure at least one photo clearly shows your face and body so there are no surprises when you meet. And don't stop at just one. Some people don't take people with one picture seriously. However, make sure the pictures are consistent with how you look.

Say, "Cheese!"

Your smile says so much about you. So don't fake your smile, or make yourself look cheesy, but also you don't want to look like the sinister Cheshire Cat.

Smile in your photo because smiling goes a long way to engage people who are looking at your profile. And if you can't smile because your teeth are yellow, get them whitened. Visit the dentist or purchase some whitening strips. Smiles create a great first impression, and put others at ease. But, don't overdo it – there's always the danger of seeming phony.

Eyes Are the Windows

If you wear glasses, then make sure you have them on in some of your photos. Sunglasses, however, are a no-no; you should not hide your eyes or face in any way. I've known people to post a blurry picture or to try and hide behind a pair of dark sunglasses. If you don't feel confident about who you are and what you look like, maybe you should work on yourself before putting yourself in the public light.

Photo Selection

I get it. You can't be objective about your pictures. I think that most people criticize themselves in photos – we know our flaws better than anyone! So ask a friend to help you pick out cute pictures or have them take some of you. Every person has a smart phone these days so there's no reason why you shouldn't have decent pictures.

And I hate those topless mirror selfies. This type of photo exhibits immaturity and/or someone only looking for sex. These guys are usually attracted to that "out there" girl who will provide him with the drama-filled relationship he craves. These pictures are known as the "Jersey Shore Shots," and nobody means that in a good way.

Ladies, censor your photos! Avoid bikini shots or showing too much skin, unless you are looking to attract stalkers or guys looking for one night stands. Don't be too seductive, it's better to send out a subtle invitation. Always remember people: Picture are forever! Once it's online, it is not coming off – just like that tramp stamp or ex's name tattooed on your body that seemed like such a good idea at the time. Here's another tip for you ladies: Men are more attracted to women in red.

Let the photos tell a story of who you are. Your photos should promote elements of your personality and the best way to do this is through the outfits and accessories you choose. Plan your outfits strategically so they reflect who you are. And yes men this goes for you as well. Women are attracted to men with a sense of style.

A final word on pictures. If you've been online dating for a while and not getting many hits, you should be updating your photos regularly. Someone may pass you by the first time but see a different photo of you the next time and be intrigued. So take some great shots of yourself and attach them to your profile – you never know who might be online!

Chapter 15

Hi! I Wanted To
Send You A Note

The great thing about online dating is you have so many pictures to look at and countless profiles to read. The drawback to online dating is that you have so many pictures to look at and countless profiles to read. However, after you've created a great profile for yourself, you'll have a better understanding of how to quickly sift through those whom you are interested in from those you are not.

So what happens next? Refine your search options to individuals in your age group and geographic location. Location, location, location! Unless you are the proud owner of a private jet, chatting with someone who lives on the opposite coast is just useless. Most dating sites will let you further refine your search to ethnicity, height, level of education, body type, children, looking for and more. Here is where things get tricky. Don't get too specific or your dating pool will soon become a pond filled with very few fish.

Let's say you've narrowed your choices down to a couple of people. It's now time to reach out! Remember, first impressions are lasting ones so make your first message a memorable one.

Use Humor

As Marilyn Monroe once said: "If you can make a girl laugh you can make her do anything."

Make the individual laugh and you will likely get a response! But avoid being cheesy, and aim your joke at something you both have in common. Perhaps something in their profile – maybe a song? How about a funny film quote?

Start with Shared Interests

Spark a conversation by talking about a mutual interest. Perhaps you have traveled to the same location, you both have dogs or maybe talk about your favorite sports team. Things in common are a great way to bridge the gap between strangers. The focus stays on your shared interest until one of you is comfortable enough to say, "So tell me about yourself."

Ask an Open-ended Question

There are two types of questions: Closed and open-ended. Closed questions require a simple yes or no answer, such as: What time do you get up for work? How long will it take you to get the restaurant? Questions that lead to a simple one-word answer can easily result in a dead-end conversation. Instead, ask an open-ended question such as: "What are some of the best concerts you've attended?" "What do you like most about this restaurant?"Asking questions is a great way to get to know someone, but there's a balance. You don't want to come across as an interrogator. So be ready to offer up unique information and insights about yourself. And please, please, please, do not suggest a face-to-face date in your first message.

Compliment Interests

No one likes getting messages from someone who has completely ignored what is written in their profile and only talks about how hot or sexy they are. Those messages are shallow and meaningless. Instead, aim your message at something referred to in their profile. Prove you have actually read it! Compliment their taste in music or perhaps tell them how interested you are in learning more about their career.

When writing a message, your goal is to pique someone's interest, have them browse your profile and if they like what they see, move forward.

Example Message 1

Hi there!

I was reading through your profile and noticed you are a huge fan of Stephen King. He has been my favorite author since the beginning of time! What is your favorite Stephen King book? Do you have any books/ authors you might recommend?

Paul

P.S. I noticed you have a horse. I grew up with horses! How often do you go riding?

Example Message 2

Hi! I liked your profile, and I was beginning to wonder if I had checked off the wrong location. So many people like "long walks on the beach" while I sit here waiting for for the snow to melt ... I was confused and jealous. LOL. I see you like Jazz and Blues music. I love Jazz and Blues! Do you know of any places that play that music? I would be very interested in knowing.

Monica

After the initial contact, don't jump into a phone conversation, unless you are sure this is something mutual. While the younger generation is more comfortable with text messages, those forty and older tend to like the sound of someone's voice. So I suggest setting up a phone conversation before meeting to give you both a level of comfort. If your time is valuable, a phone conversation is a great way to be efficient. When I was dating, there were a couple times I was on the phone with someone and thought: "I can't possibly meet this person!"

An individual's voice says a lot about them. Sometimes, if you have not dated for a long while, or have been looking for a while, your judgment becomes impaired because you just want to meet someone. Instead of rushing into a meeting, get a better sense of who they are and how they carry themselves. Whatever comes out of their mouth could totally turn you on or off, then you can take your next step. I often remind my clients that it can be difficult knowing what to talk about so having conversations with strangers as an activity will help you raise your level of comfort.

Weeding Through The Duds

*K*nowing what you want helps you find those searching for the same. Are you looking for a serious relationship or casual dating? With thousands of potential people to meet online, not everyone has the same intentions as you. Sometimes, "the advertisement" can be misleading. In order to be successful, you must be able to identify any red flags in a user's profile. The less time you waste with unsuitable candidates, the more time you have for yourself and the less jaded you will become with your overall online dating experience. Dating can get tiring if you're meeting all the wrong people. If this happens, take a break for a while.

When dating online, you need to be aware of any warning signals in an individual's profile – if you spot any of the below, then proceed with caution.

Here is a guide that will help you weed out unsavory candidates so you can use your time efficiently to hunt down the good ones.

Mr. or Mrs. Unavailable

This person has recently left a marriage or long-term relationship and is looking for someone to fill a void and unload their baggage. I always advise an individual to remain single at least six months to a year after leaving a lengthy relationship. A word of advice: If you contact someone and find out they've been single for less than three months – proceed with caution! These people can be emotionally, mentally and spiritually unavailable, and you may find yourself in a caretaker role. Having said this, if you feel the two of you are compatible, all is not lost; just go slow. He or she might not be fully over an ex, but if their hopes of reconciliation have been exhausted it is possible that all they need is a good partner.

"The best way to get over someone is to get under someone else." True?

Yes and No. Connecting with someone is a great way to move past a failed relationship – if you are truly ready. However, you don't want to have a "rebound" relationship just to make you feel better.

It is important to realize that the healing process can be complex and lengthy. Following a separation, women feel an immediate emotional sting while men suffer intensely over a long period. A 2015 Binghampton University study shows that "women experience more emotional pain following a breakup, but they also fully recover." Men on the other hand "never fully recover–they just move on… and will likely feel the loss deeply and for a long period of time as it "sinks in" that he must "start competing" all over again to replace what he has lost–or worse still, come to the realization that the loss is irreplaceable."[9]

Dealing with a break-up leaves men feeling injured and beaten. Women, understand that men are more obsessive. Men view their women as possessions or the trophy after winning the big game.

---

9   Binghampton University, Press Release; Study: Women Hurt More by Breakups but Recover More Fully, August 11, 2015
    http://www.binghamton.edu/mpr/news-releases/news-release.html?id=2315

Because of this, they have a harder time letting go. Men, understand that women, in general, are emotionally driven by relationships, After pouring herself into her past man, she needs time to recharge her "relationship battery."

One or No Photo Wonder

This individual only has one photo posted and refuses to send you more. With cell phone cameras readily available, Mr. or Ms. One Picture Wonder has no excuses not to post or make additional pictures available. If they don't, it is not a good sign and if they say they do not have any friends, that's even worse!

There is always the possibility that the person is too shy, but online dating requires a certain degree of disclosure. However, if they are unwilling to show who they truly are, that person shouldn't be on an online dating site. No one buys a pair of shoes or clothing online without seeing photos, color and size, right?

Be wary of the one, or no-photo individual. The picture they display might have been poached off someone else's profile, or it may even be some hot celebrity. Just move on.

Example: Carlos goes online and starts chatting with Carina, who has no picture attached with her profile, but offers the illusion of being extremely sensual and sexy. She keeps ignoring the photo comments from Carlos and he eventually stops asking to see them. The pair take their conversation offline and start talking on the phone. Excitement builds as he waits for their first meeting, a coffee date. He is going in completely blind yet open-minded. Not knowing who he's looking for, he wanders through the café, hopeful, then hears a voice calling to him. Carina knew what he looked like from the several pictures Carlos had posted. Here is his story:

She was shockingly unattractive and my mouth dropped open. Despite this I felt I had to give her a chance. I had no out and she knew what I looked like, so I went to sit down. Unfortunately, my level of acceptance maxed-out very early. Not only was she unattractive, she was obnoxious too.

My butt sprung up from the chair and I said, "I can't take this anymore, no wonder you didn't post a picture! You look like someone whose parents were related before they got married." She naturally became defensive and replied, "Yeah well you are shorter than you said." She was furious, and left.

Don't waste your time on someone who doesn't have at least three photos of themselves. Taking and sending photos is so easy and if an individual does not use technology, they are probably living in ancient times and unwilling to evolve.

The Perpetual Pen-Pal

Naturally you want to move the relationship from technology to real life. A good rule of thumb is three to four emails. If he or she does not ask to meet by then, either you move on – or you ask them out.

Example: Kristin is a professional, who is looking for the same. She is highly ambitious and finds she has no time to meet men in a social environment. After hearing of her many friends who were online dating, Kristin threw caution to the wind and tried the same. Jason was one of her first online conversations.

Kristin was eager to meet Jason. They started chatting when he was in the city on business but a meet-up failed to materialize. When he returned home, they continued speaking and he assured her that he would visit soon. He was only a two-hour drive away, but the miles between them started to grow. Their daily chats kept her engaged but his constant "soon" started to drive her away. Four months later, he finally drove in for a quick dinner. Much to her disappointment, although he looked like his photos, his character and the way he carried himself was nothing like she envisioned. For Kristen, it was four months of waiting, only to experience a classic case of anticipation-is-greater-than-realization syndrome.

Here is her story: *I was so excited over meeting him that first time! It turned out to be a huge failure but I am happy I found out without having to go another four months. I was good about it, and even paid the dinner bill to thank him for making the drive to see me. He wasn't what*

I expected but still a nice guy, and because we had connected in that time we continue to be friends. But, I will never, ever let it happen again. No more developing relationships online. Just face-to-face.

Kristin now has strict rules. A maximum of three chats and then the meet. No exceptions.

Avoid lengthy online conversations and people who avoid conversation about meeting, or are always too busy. We all make time for things we really want to do, and those stragglers are wasting your time.

Not sure how to handle this kind of character? Tell them that you are not interested in a pen pal and you'd like to meet sooner rather than later.

If arrangements are not made soon after, move on. He or she could be married, just looking for online company, or worse, they may be buttering you up to play some con. Ladies, I promise you, he's not a Nigerian Prince! This is quite common these days because technology has made it easier for people to hide behind their computers where they don't actually have to socialize in a real-life environment. People sit in the comfort of their homes, playing on their phones or computers, knowing they don't have to go out. So be serious about who and what you are looking for. Impose that rule of communicating three or four times.

No-Shirt, Half-Naked Selfies

Ladies, if you have been on an online dating site, you know this type of guy. Men, how many half-naked photos of women have you seen?

If an individual is prepared to post half-naked mirror selfies or suggestive bikini photos online for the world to see, what else will he or she be prepared to do? If this is the kind of individual you are drawn to, then you are in for a world of hurt.

Always avoid profiles with the no-shirt guy or the lying-on-a-bed-in-a-bikini girl! Sure, a photo of him or her on a beach, or on vacation, is fine. But if every photo of them is half-naked or in front of a bathroom mirror, then there is something wrong.

This type of individual is seemingly confident, but reality says they are stuck on themselves. They can also be insecure and immature. A word of caution: Half-naked photos scream, "I don't have anything else to offer other than my body."

What other types of photos come with a major warning signal?

- The individual who Photoshops out the ex. If it is the only decent picture he or she has, they're not taking online dating seriously. There could also be some heavy baggage they are lugging around.
- People with the old photos. Their profile says they are 42, but they look like they are 22 in the pictures. I've said it before and it bears repeating: Posted pictures should be no more than a year old. People who post pictures from 20 years ago are not living in reality.

The Repeat Offender

He or she showers you with compliments and tells you how excited they are to meet you, but then goes off the grid and disappears. And just when you think they are gone, he or she returns with a, "Hey there!"

This individual has no intention of meeting you, but if you have not spoken with anyone significant since, you will likely give them another chance. No second chances! Just delete and block. I've been there, and these individuals are serious time-sucking vampires.

Inappropriate Screen Names

Creating a catchy user name is just as important as choosing a great photo. Go for profiles that show a sense of creativity – the playful or witty usernames. The names reflect something about their personality, so select with care! Avoid those that are overtly sexual or overall inappropriate. Don't go for profiles with names that are too risqué.

Examples of red-flag usernames:

- *BigJunk4You*: Excuse me? I don't want your "junk" and don't care how it is sized.
- *JustKidding*: Yeah and you must be kidding if you think I will ever take you seriously.
- *Imhisforever*: Hmmm, not too forward, are we?
- *PhunPhucker*: This one leaves me speechless.
- *KeepMeHard:* No thank you.
- *TongueLasher:* Again, no thank you.

Status: Separated

If someone says they are separated you have to find out *how* separated they are. Some individuals live under the same roof as their ex, or they've just recently separated and are still scraping through the paperwork to make it official. That kind of situation is just a headache. If there's still another man or woman involved to any degree, there will be drama. Stay clear.

Incomplete Bio

You'll often see people with non-descript, or incomplete bios.

- o "I am just here checking this out, will write more later."
- o "Looking to make some new friends. You in?"
- o "Datable and fantastic."

This kind of profile, or lack thereof, should make you question if the individual is really serious about the whole process and developing a relationship. Keep in mind, though, that people often revise and update their profiles, so keep an open mind if this happens. But until then, skip over it.

Tunnel Vision

Who isn't looking for Mr. or Ms. Perfect. But what does "perfect" mean? We all have our own versions.

When it comes to physical attraction, we can have tunnel vision. However, those who are fixated on physical appearance can be insecure and way too demanding, with a huge checklist of the type of person they desire.

"You have to be an athletic or slim woman. I'm extremely athletic, and I don't want anyone with a few extra pounds."

"You must be independent and not the kind of man who expects a woman to care for you."

"I like my women put together, ones who dress really well and look hot in high heels."

"I don't want a woman who is judgmental."

"Unless you're a business executive, don't bother contacting me."

These opening lines can lead into a laundry list of particulars.

Individuals who include these kinds of statements are high maintenance and impossibly picky. They also may have gone through a bad divorce or relationship, and they are hurting – bad. Or, they are looking to avoid any resemblance to their ex. These individuals will berate you the second you gain one pound, miss out on a raise at work, or choose to wear track pants to fill the car up with gas.

The Ego

"I, I, I, me, me, me." This is the individual who likes to talk about themselves, only about themselves, and always about themselves. He or she feels they are better than the rest. (The truth is this person is extremely insecure and needs constant attention.) This person is very specific with wants and won't settle for anything else. They make themselves sound like an amazing catch, but usually he or she is one of those fish you quickly want to toss back into the water!

Let's Talk About Sex, Baby!

"I don't like going out, why don't I come over to your place? I bet we can have some serious fun together."

Be wary of the person who immediately starts talking about sex, using sexual innuendos, or takes you off the dating site to text and send you inappropriate pictures. Pass!

Shouldn't, Wouldn't, Can't or Don't

If you come across anyone who uses these words, the individual is really telling you he or she may be damaged goods:

"I won't accept that again."
"I shouldn't allow that."
"I can't handle this or that."
"I don't like people who can't handle my type of personality."

This individual paints a picture of negativity and may be too jaded by the past to really move forward. This type of person? You shouldn't, wouldn't, can't and don't do!

Kids Are My Priority

Really? You have children and they are your priority? If anyone says children are number one – run! Of course children are incredibly important; we all understand that, but you have to accept that you will always be number two. However, the focus should be on the current relationship because without that, there is no commitment.

How To Spot A Scammer

$\mathcal{I}$'m sure you've heard of a Ponzi scheme. These are businesses set up to create wealth for those at the top at the expense of those on the ground floor. And when the money stops flowing in, the business collapses, and the majority of people lose their entire investment. These can also be called "scammer" businesses.

Online dating has its shares of scammers as well. With so many options, and so many people appearing to be real, it is hard to really know if you are being baited by a *catfish* (definition: "Someone who falsely takes on the identity of real people"). Even the smartest people can fall prey to these people; they seem sincere, sweet and are very attentive. These online Ponzi imposters scheme to win you over. They tap into your sympathies with sad stories and shower you with loving words, with the goal of spending all of your money and controlling all of your time. According to ScamWatch.com, a consumer taskforce in Australia that identifies scams across the country, more than 2,600 individuals were caught in online dating scams, with an estimated financial loss of $23 million; 39 percent of the scammers were identified as male and 43.5 percent were female.[10]

Warning Signs

- ☻ They say they are God-fearing people.
- ☻ Their profile sounds too romantic. They use a lot of cliches, tender talk with promises of endless love, and make you think they can whisk you away to fairy tale land.
- ☻ Too eager to get to know you too quickly.
- ☻ They write things like: "I'm looking for true love and marriage." Come on! Normal people don't talk like that.
- ☻ They don't video chat.
- ☻ They always have an excuse not to meet. Mostly a sick family member, financial turmoil or personal illness.
- ☻ Sometimes they use a picture of a famous person as their profile photo. Here's a tip: If you are not sure about photos, you can do a photo check. You can save an image and place it into Google Image search to determine if that picture is marked as a scammer or a legitimate picture.
- ☻ They use words like loyal and honest a lot in their profile. Almost all scammers say they are honest.
- ☻ They use bad grammar.
- ☻ Always look for inconsistencies. If they say they are 6'1", there is no way they can only be 100lbs.
- ☻ They prey on the elderly, the lonely, and the vulnerable. Here's something to keep in mind: One of my matchmaking clients, John Mageau, is the victim of ongoing online dating scams. His identity was stolen over ten years ago and these Internet scammers continue to create fake accounts with stolen images from his online dating profile. They have been successful at scamming women from around the globe

---

10 Australian Competition and Consumer Commission, Smart Watch; Dating & Romance Statistics (Scams), 2015 numbers, https://www.scamwatch.gov.au/ types-of-scams/dating-romance

out of thousands of dollars. To avoid having your identity stolen, John suggests that you don't post more than three images of yourself on your profile. It's been a rough road for John; he's been featured as a scammer on television programs in various countries including the UK and as a result, has had a difficult time maintaining a relationship. I know he's innocent and I'm over the moon excited for him; he recently met what he calls "the one" at a Single in the City speed dating event.

🖐 Most often they live miles from you. They say they are widowed, in the army, or always traveling on business.

Don't let these people turn you away from online dating. Always remember to be smart when searching. Trust your instincts if you see red flags. You can also have a friend read over a profile, if you are not sure.

From Dating To Relationship

*Y*ou made it! You've poured through countless profiles, or perhaps you came across someone interesting right away. Either way, you are ready to start dating! You've texted or talked on the phone, and you're both excited about finally meeting in person. You are about to go out for dinner with the individual who sparked your interest. Yes, you are a bit nervous because, well, this is groundbreaking for you – dating outside your comfort zone. Your mind even wanders a little bit: What if she's nuts? What if he's wearing ugly shoes? What if she's overweight? What if he's not as cute as he looks in his pictures? What if he has food stuck in his teeth? Do I tell him?

In this final section, we're going to look at what to do and not do, and what you can expect when dating. The goal? To help you move to a second, third, and forth date, and to what you've been looking for all along – a long-term relationship, including marriage!

That First Date

The First Date

Okay, you've connected with Mr. Handsome or Ms. Hottie. You've agreed on a date, but you are so nervous! *What do I say? How do I act? What are we going to talk about?* These and a host of other questions go through our minds when we are getting ready for date #1.

My first response to you is *r-e-l-a-x*. The other person is equally anxious and also wants to connect with you, the real you. So chill out and be yourself! That's right, be yourself.

Don't overdo the alcohol in an attempt to calm your nerves. Limit your consumption so you don't get out of hand, leaving a bad impression.

Men and women can both come across as too forceful or forward. Men like to feel like they're in control and need to be protectors and providers. As a woman you don't need a man to tell you what to do, but he'll be more attracted to you if you allow him his manly gallantries, like suggesting a place to meet or paying for dinner.

What happens if you decide to meet someplace and haven't met the other person already? This can present a problem. You're looking around the restaurant for him or her, but you're not really sure who you're looking for, except for the online picture you've seen. So be prepared for some unexpected scenarios, and extend some courtesy if needed.

Example: *Vinnie had been chatting with Zoya, a woman he met online. Zoya seemed very nice and they had some great conversations. When it was time to finally meet, Vinnie arrived at their selected restaurant at 6:55 p.m. for their 7 p.m. date, and waited for her to arrive.*

At 7:05, Zoya called him. "You're late!" she said, harshly. She hadn't realized he was already there. By using that tone, she was demonstrating signs of dominance, inflexibility and selfishness.

Despite her abrupt behavior, Vinnie searched everywhere for her. He even went so far as to pulling out her photo and asking the waiter if he had seen her. The waiter told him there was a lady waiting for him at a corner table. Vinnie looked over at her and was shocked over her weight. He took a deep breath, and decided to give her a chance, wanting to make the most of this date. After getting over some initial awkwardness, Vinnie settled in. He was friendly and told jokes that she found so funny that coffee streamed from her nose, back in to her cup - super attractive! But he had to cut the date short. Not because he was a thoughtless donkey, but because he had to go to the wake of a friend's mother, who had died suddenly. He didn't want to cancel the date with Zoya because he was a gracious man and was actually looking forward to meeting her. After a short hour, he let Zoya know he had to leave.

When Vinnie returned home from the wake about 9:15 p.m., there was a text message from Zoya: "You butthole. I can't believe you would use the excuse of your friend's dead mother." In response, Vinnie replied with a photo of the woman who passed away. She quickly apologized but he was done. His last message to her said: "Lose my number." He didn't feel the need to be gracious anymore.

Lesson for all: Don't be too brash, impatient, or self-focused! There's a fine line between assertive and aggressive, and the latter will surely drive people away.

It is normal to have the jitters on a first date. But don't forget he or she is probably nervous too. Realizing that may calm you a little.

Also, realize the first date does not have to be a spectacular display of fireworks. Give this first date a chance to develop. Quite often the best relationships are the ones that gradually blossom into something real and beautiful, as opposed to the instant connections that start with a blaze and soon fade into ashes.

If your first date is not absolutely amazing, but has its positive moments, give that person another chance. Often, the second date is exponentially less nerve-wracking, providing you the opportunity to notice the real person. You may even really like what you discover.

Lesson for all: Don't be too brash, impatient, or self-focused! There's a fine line between assertive and aggressive, and the latter will surely drive people away.

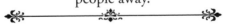

First Date Guidelines

As a matchmaker, I always look at hobbies and preferences. Do both people like to play pool? Hit golf balls at the range? These comfortable environments put people at ease in their own element and gives them something to talk about. They are not your ordinary "let's go for dinner or drinks or coffee." Activity-based dates provide a great opportunity for engaging conversation, allowing daters with shared interests to be more relaxed.

Most importantly, if are you not attracted to the person you are with, you will still be doing something you enjoy.

Always keep your first date short, and I strongly urge you to implement my *One Hour Date Rule*. If you're both having a great time, save that excitement for date two! Don't give up too much too quickly so that you can keep your date longing for more.

The One Hour Date Rule also works magic if there is no compatibility. It protects you from overextending the date, getting too personal too quickly and being stuck with someone you really do not like.

Example: *Chatting online for some time, Roger and Mindy finally decided to take their relationship offline and into the real world. They decided to meet at a halfway point between their homes, about a thirty-minute drive for each. As Mindy is driving to meet Roger, he calls and says he forgot his wallet. No problem, she thought. It would be a cheap date, even if she had to pay. They were only meeting for a drink. Her covering his tab would be easier, saving them both the time of having to wait while he returned home to grab his wallet.*

The initial contact was incredible. He was full of apologies and compliments. The pair sat in a booth to watch a hockey game, and then it started. Beer and lots of it for Roger, flowing from the Mindy tap. (He obviously wasn't too concerned about drinking and driving. A huge sign of irresponsibility or an experienced scam artist!)

But it wasn't just the beer. Along with drinking, Roger got the worst case of the munchies and Mindy was too shy to not allow him to order food. At the end of the date, Mindy suggested he take her out the next time. The pair texted but the relationship soon fizzled into a memory.

If Mindy had enforced my *One Hour First Date Rule*, she would not have accumulated such a large bill with a guy she'd never see again.

Here are some One Hour First Date Ideas:

- 🐚 Go for a smoothie or healthy juice
- 🐚 Grab a snack and sit in a park
- 🐚 Grab a coffee and go for a walk
- 🐚 Visit an ice-cream parlor
- 🐚 Take your dogs to a dog park
- 🐚 Visit a farmers market
- 🐚 Grab breakfast or an express lunch

Helpful Tips

- 🐚 Do yoga or workout in the morning, or a couple of hours before the date, to keep you relaxed throughout the day.
- 🐚 Listen to music, dance around and work off some energy! Enjoy a glass of wine or one cocktail – not three or four. The last thing you want to do is slur through your introduction or share stories that lack any sense.
- 🐚 *Be prepared.* Think of interesting things to talk about to avoid that awkward silence. No need to memorize anything but have a sense of what's going on in the world. Skim the newspaper, watch the news, read some articles. Having questions on the tip of your tongue will help with conversation and let you find out more about the other person's views and opinions.
- 🐚 A reminder: Ask open-ended questions!
- 🐚 Listen to what is being said, and respond with relevant information or ask questions related to the topic. Also know when to speak and when to listen. It's a two-way street; make sure you both get airtime.
- 🐚 There's a fine line between maintaining eye contact and staring at someone. It's okay to look away when you're both in conversation as this is a normal thing to do. Just don't be paying more attention to someone or something else. The moment your eyes start wandering, you are showing signs of disinterest or boredom.

@ Approach your date with a positive attitude. If you are not in the mood to share some time with someone, then politely ask if you can postpone. Be respectful of their time and make sure you reschedule well in advance.

@ Maintain good posture and watch your body language.

Not Sure What To Talk About?

I understand that it's easy for your mind to go blank or to get tongue-tied. After all, you don't want to get foot-in-mouth sickness! Here are some things to help you move the conversations along:

1. What do you like to do? What are your hobbies or what do you like to do in your spare time? Hobbies can tell a lot about a person and if you have common interests.
2. Where were you born? Where did you grow up?
3. What kind of sports do you like playing or watching?
4. What kind of pets do you have? Those who have pets are usually very passionate about them. This could lead to a fun and entertaining conversation.
5. If you could change places with anyone in the world for a day who would you be and why?
6. What if you won the lottery what would you do with the money? Find out about their character in a light-hearted way.
7. What sort of books do you like to read? Have you ever read a book that changed your life?
8. If you could live anywhere in the world, where would it be and why?
9. What do you think of reality TV? What would you do if you were approached and asked to be a contestant in a reality show? Learn about their character; are they an introvert or extrovert?
10. What's the most amazing place you've ever been? Learn about your date's life experiences and passions with this simple question that offers the chance for an ample response.

11. Where were you on September 11, 2001? Everyone remembers this day and where they were.
12. Did you hear what's going on with _____? (Talk about something trending in the news and stay away from religion and politics.)
13. What's your favorite kind of food/or favorite restaurant?
14. What genre of movie is your favorite?
15. What are some of the things on your bucket list? Have your list ready, have fun comparing ideas and notes.

Guys, Converse With Her!

I know guys who can recite the passing statistics of every quarterback in the NFL. I know other guys who can tear an engine apart, name every piece, and put it back together again, as if it were a kid's building block set. But these same guys can't hold a conversation about current events, the latest trends, or anything else outside of their favorite topic. Guys, women like to converse, and they want to talk to you! So step out of your comfort zone and find out what's going on in the world. Both you and your date will greatly benefit!

First Date Precautions

If you are a serial first-time dater – meaning you've had many first dates but very few second ones – I can offer you some advice to help you make it to date two, three, and four, and possibly a lasting relationship. After many years of working as a dating coach, I've discovered there are some key things that can completely turn off your date. Both men and women are attracted to people who are genuine, natural and sincere. If you're trying to make it to the second date, be conscious of these dating no-no's.

Bragging

Don't be that grandstanding boastful person. It's great that you have achieved so much in life, but never let your ego take control. Unless you are looking for a gold digger, little time should be spent on conversations about finances. It rarely impresses. In fact, it usually does the opposite; most people think the more someone brags about financial success, the more that person lacks in other departments. And don't go boasting about how popular you are in the online dating world! This is a huge turn-off. You're basically telling people that you've dated everyone online and are still single, so, maybe you are less the prize and more a party favor?

Preoccupied

Although cell phones play a critical role in meeting people, they can damage a relationship if you are phone obsessed. It's never okay to be on the phone and checking your Facebook or Twitter, or texting friends when you're on a date. That's just rude. It takes away from quality, face-to-face time, and there is no reason to be documenting your date on Snapchat or Instagram. Taking out your cell phone shows that you are not too interested in your present company or that you feel the date is not going well.

There are exceptions to this phone rule. If you have been with someone for a while, or have to take a work-related call, it can be acceptable. Always be thoughtful and explain why the call is so important: "Please excuse me, but I've got a really important call coming through at 7:30. I was looking forward to our date and didn't want to cancel because of this call."

Under no circumstances should anyone have casual conversations with friends, who want to know "What's up!" Trust me, this happens, too often.

Example: *I met this one guy at a restaurant lounge for appetizers and cocktails and I was hopeful. This guy was handsome, he smelled good, seemed to be a gentleman, very complimentary and he really seemed to fancy me. But once we got to the lounge he completely changed. He was on his phone the entire time, either texting or calling, and laughing with his friends. He didn't seem to notice I was getting more and more angry. Finally, he got off the phone and boldy said: "I'm renovating my house right now. Want to see some pictures of the stripper pole I'm adding into the games room?"*

I was so shocked that I got up and left. He had such an attitude that he didn't even try stop me as I walked out the door. Obviously he had no respect for women, or me, and he was a total jerk. Actually, I wouldn't be surprised if there was nobody on the other end of the texts or phone calls; he just didn't have the maturity to pull off being on a date and having a conversation with an actual woman. I don't think he was serious about really meeting someone.

Maybe he has some insecurity issues or he's just plain clueless. He thought what he was doing was funny, but – who asks a girl if she wants to see his stripper pole on a first date? He doesn't get it. He's rude.

He did call and text me after, but I ignored him. He had his chance and he blew it. Those are the kind of things that happen that are not negotiable, because it shows his character. If he can do that to me on a first date, what other stupid things would he do?

The phone might help you find the date, but it has no place *on* a first date!

TMI

A Note for Guys: So the other night, you and your buddies drank so much that you tea-bagged your best friend while he was passed out, and you weren't sure who that "chick" was in bed next to you the morning after. Or, you were recently diagnosed as bipolar or you once broke your pelvic bone after crashing to the ground when your newly installed sex swing unhinged.

Come on, guys. No respectful woman wants to hear they are dating an over-aged frat boy. Be reserved when you are on your first date and don't share too much information.

Lesson: Watch what you say! Too much information too early on in the dating phase can completely kill your chances.

Something for Women: I was dating this guy that I thought I really fancied and after our second date we got into a conversation about New Year's Eve. He told me that he was going to Vegas with his buddies. I mentioned that because of my hectic New Year's party every year, I would actually appreciate and expect the guy I'm dating to come and help me out at the party. He stopped taking my calls and I had no clue as to why.

I ran into him a couple of months later and he told me the reason he cut off communication was that he wasn't changing his New Year's plans with the guys and could foresee a future problem between the two of us. Lesson: Watch what you say! Too much information too early on in the dating phase can completely kill your chances.

Tardiness

Being late shows that you do not value anyone else's time but your own. Having your date wait only sets a bad tone for the evening, so make an extra effort to be a little early. Show that special person that you are responsible and that you appreciate their time.

Example: *I once dated a firefighter who was always late for our dates. I'm not talking five or ten minutes late, but up to three hours. Yes, crazy! I really liked him and wanted to get to know him better but his tardiness created a negative tone for our dates. I just assumed he was always late for everything. One day I asked him, "As a firefighter, how can you show up late for work but don' t lose your job?"*

"He replied, "Oh, I'm never late for work.""

So he's never late for work but always late for me. Hmmm, that just showed me that he was disrespectful of my time. He valued his time, but not mine. I gave him plenty of warnings not to be late for future dates and to respect my time, but he continued his habit. Finally I broke up with him. He begged for me to come back, and tried for four years; he thought I was the best thing that happened to him.

I'm sure you get my point. Pay attention when your date tells you something, and don't dismiss it. You may end up regretting it for a long time, or who knows, maybe forever.

Negativity

Whoa! Buzz killer.

Example: *After online dating for almost four years, Suzzie told me that she had run the gamut of men. There was a guy whom she really connected with in their online conversations. But, when they finally met, not only did he look different from his pictures, but he spent the entire date talking about how unattractive he was and how women always rejected him. At this point, Meryl Streep would have had a hard time acting surprised that women rejected him. He also went on about his ex and how he believed she was never really in love with him.*

Their date got even more interesting when he started asking Suzzie for advice, and she couldn't get out of there quick enough. Then he asked, straight out, if Suzzie thought he was ugly! She didn't know what to say!

After all that, they guy had the nerve to ask her out on another date! Sure, she felt really bad for him – the poor guy was insecure so she didn't want to beat him down any further. So she skirted this question by saying she would think about it.

After not hearing from him for a few days, and thinking she was in the clear, Suzzie received an email from him. But, this email didn't say a thing. All he did was send a picture of his penis; at least she assumed it was his. Nevertheless, she was shocked to say the least.

Enough said.

Sex, Anyone?

It still blows me away when I hear some of the conversations people feel are appropriate.

Guys, most women are not turned on by men who talk about how many women they've had sex with or how they would love to be deep-throated in the bathroom, "hint hint…." Women are so tired of being propositioned by men so leave the sexual innuendos for when you know her better.

Ladies, most of you are not looking for a one-night stand. So don't lead your guy on. Talking about sex on the first date will give him the wrong impression – of you!

Sweeten the Deal

So now that we've discussed first date repellents, let's talk about how you can win his or her heart.

Guys, first and foremost, a little gift, like flowers or perhaps a book written by her favorite author, will be greatly appreciated. Women love to be complimented and to know that their efforts are being recognized. Tell her she looks really great or that there is something about her outfit that you really like.

Ladies, be sure to say something about the way he looks or is dressed. Small compliments are a great way to open his heart when you first meet.

Be Attentive

It's true that men and women speak different languages – and men are just not programmed to listen. (Feel free to re-read the chapter about communication.)

Many women do judge men based on their ability to listen and engage. It's important to understand that women are communicators and they can quickly make a connection with a man who listens, and talks, but not just about himself. After all, you're having a conversation, not performing a monologue.

Being nervous is natural, but don't let yourself be overly rattled that conversation is so dull, or falls into a state of silence, that he or she is looking for an exit. Ask her about herself and the things she enjoys. Show some excitement in his hobbies and interests, even if you don't know anything about them. And if you want to see that person again, suggest a second date, perhaps one that involves one of their passions, like dancing or attending a concert or sports event. Always be respectful and move forward at a pace you are both comfortable with. Being too forceful can scare him or her off. Just a sweet goodnight will leave them yearning for more.

Flirt! Flirt! Flirt!

Did I get your attention? Everyone loves a little flirting.

Before you get too physical, make sure you are correctly reading his or her body language. Guys, she might want you to move in a little closer or take her hand and give her subtle touches. Maybe a kiss the end of the date. (When I say kiss at the end of the date, I mean a sweet, gentle kiss. Don't shove your tongue down her throat like you're trying to taste her tonsils; that's an excellent way to ensure there will be no second date!) If, however, she is not sending positive body language, back off and don't invade her personal space. Many people are very mindful of their space and having a stranger, especially a man, come too close can be invasive and distressing. Don't get close unless she gives you that invitation.

Positive body language:

- ☺ They move or lean in closer to you: They find you interesting and are comfortable with you in their personal space.
- ☺ They are relaxed and not sitting with their arms crossed: They are comfortable in letting their guard down.

- There are long periods of eye contact broken by moments of looking down and away due to shyness; they enjoy looking into your eyes, but at the same time it makes them a little nervous. Butterflies, anyone?
- The smiles and laughs are genuine (women tend to giggle a lot), your conversation is found to be engaging and interesting. Guys, she lets you know by licking her lips or twirling her hair.

Signs to back off:

- They move or lean away from you and might even choose to sit across the table to give themselves some distance. When this happens quickly understand that they do not want you near them.
- Crossed arms: Remember when you were a little kid and you were asked to do something you hated? Your first reaction was likely to cross your arms in defiance. Crossed arms can – but not always – indicate a person is physically cold, closed off, or frustrated. Or it can even indicate that they've simply had too much to eat.
- Looking away: Either they are bored or do not find you interesting enough to watch.
- His/her feet are pointed away from you, or towards the exit; they are looking for an escape.

A single cue can mean a number of things, so it's necessary to pay close attention to multiple behavioral indicators. While it will help determine their comfort level, you will have to dig a little deeper to really understand the signals being delivered. This means paying attention to what they are really saying.

Pick Up the Tab

Listen up guys, here's my general rule: If you ask a woman out, you should pay for at least the first date. If she asks you out but you really like her, you should still pay for the date. If she asks you out and you're not interested at the end of the date, then you can do whatever you'd like.

I don't usually recommend dinners for first-time daters. If you have met her and are trying to impress her, a nice dinner will give you bonus points. Otherwise, it's always best if you do coffee, drinks, or try one of my *One Hour First Date Ideas* (refer to Chapter 18) to spare yourself having to spend time with someone you do not like. Some women can feel uncomfortable when eating in front of a man for the first time. And remember, if you are dating a lot, then this can get pricey!

Ladies, we know we would like the guy to pick up the first, maybe the second tab, but don't just expect it – at least pull your wallet out. If you are going out with him a second time, show your appreciation by bringing him something small. This could be as simple as a little box of chocolates or even better, win him over with some home baked chocolate chip cookies.

When I was dating, I made an exception for a guy I liked. After meeting online, we spent many weeks chatting with one another. He wanted to take me to one of his favorite restaurants, a half an hour away from where I live.

On the night of our date, he picked me up at my home. The only reason I allowed this was because we had mutual friends. (Guys, don't offer to pick a woman up at their home. You want to come across as someone who is safe and respectable. There are too many stalkers out there today, and you don't want to raise any suspicions.) I felt comfortable with him after our many conversations and because of our mutual friend, who had nothing bad to say about him.

He lived far away from me, and after the drive to my home he was tired and asked if we could go somewhere closer. He just didn't feel like going all the way out to his favorite restaurant and bringing me back.

At the restaurant, we ordered our food, then three drinks – along with two checks. He asked the waiter to split the bill! That was a very classy move: Not.

Without debating the two-check decision, and with the song "Hey Big Spender" stuck in my head like an earworm, we put down our cash. After he put down a $20, ...

He then asked the waitress for some change, finally paid his half of the bill, and as we were leaving, he asked if I could drive his car back. He felt a little tipsy after having two drinks – so dainty (note the sarcasm).

Obviously, I chose to take him up on that offer and drive home because I feared for my life. I drove myself back to my place and there was that awkward moment – for him – where he waited for my invitation into my house. But that just was not going to happen. He only had two drinks, no doubt he was still sober, and was just looking for a way to creep into my home.

I was thinking: Let me get this right. You ask me out on a date. We have mutual friends but you're not the least bit embarrassed to ask the waiter to split the bill. You make me pay for my own food and drinks and you top that off by asking me for money to help you cover your own bill?

I said a quick goodbye and closed the door behind me. He lacked those gentleman-like qualities that every woman looks for in a man! I was very much looking forward to a conversation with our mutual friend the next day; he was going to get an earful!

What Did I Miss?

Now let's say you went on a first date and you both had a great time. You're sure you were getting all the right cues indicating interest, but when you call or text you get a delayed response, or worse, no response at all. You're confused, you thought they liked you; your jokes were appreciated, they were very attentive, you had great conversations, what happened?

There could be a few reasons; perhaps there was genuine attraction but after giving it much thought, there is the realization of the undeniable non-negotiables that outweighed the initial attraction, i.e., you may have traits reminiscent of an ex. Or it could simply be a realization that it was too soon to date, that the sting of a past relationship was all too present.

Whatever the reason, if you call or text a couple of times and get no response, get over yourself and move on, there are other people out there who are more suitable!

Next Date No-No's

Remember, if the date doesn't work out, then chalk it up to experience. You'll learn and grow, and be able to figure out what you like and what you don't.

If a second, third, or forth date is in the works, don't get complacent! Complacency is the same as taking a person for granted, and will doom any budding relationship. Keep these "do not" pointers in mind for early and future dates:

- *Packing on the cologne/perfume.* We want to entice our date, not suffocate them.
- *Conduct an interview.* Do not grill your date.
- *Poor manners.* Swearing, picking your teeth or licking your fingers are not a good first impression.
- *Make elaborate plans.* Early dates are meant to be relatively casual. You don't want to over plan and make your date feel uncomfortable.
- *Plan a movie date.* If you're not talking, you can't get to know someone.
- *Have in-depth discussions about having children.* You want to know if the two of you have chemistry and compatibility. This is not the time to get into a serious relationship discussion.
- *Not eat.* Early dates can be nerve racking but picking at your food is only going to confuse your date and make them think you really don't want to be there.

(Y) *Check out other people/flirt with people.* Focus on your date.

(Y) *Don't be creepy postdate.* Resist the urge to immediately add your date to social media or text them non-stop.

Remember, if the date doesn't work out, then chalk it up to experience. You'll learn and grow, and be able to figure out what you like and what you don't.

Section 6

Early Relationships

The early stages of dating are exciting. Chemistry. Attraction. Conversation. Connection. Excitement at the thought of him or her. The smile that spreads across your lips when you the read a text message or hear their voice on the phone. This is what you've been looking for – and waiting for! Congratulations come from your closest friends.

Let's take a look at what happens early on in a relationship, so that you're well prepared to move even deeper.

I'm In Love! Or Is It Like?

*I*t's easy to get caught up in the relationship during the early stages; and that's the way it should be. But let's come down to earth just a little. How *should* you be acting in the early times? My advice: Slow down a little. Enjoy these days, but keep your eyes and ears open, and your wits about you.

Here's a truth: We are all on our best behavior at the beginning of a relationship. Typically, it takes about ninety days – or until "being comfortable" sets in – before the "true self" begins to emerge. Entering a new relationship isn't like tearing the wrapper off a birthday gift. You have to take your time and enjoy the excitement before seeing what's in there.

Yes, it's normal to want to spend every waking minute with your special person. However, the relationship can quickly end if you or your partner feels that the mystery has already disappeared. It's important to retain your own space and time, and continue to be happy and independent until the two of you have established a solid relationship.

Do you ever notice that the ones we really like don't necessarily like us, and the ones we aren't attracted to are the same ones who like us? One reason is that the guy or girl we like, we can pay too much attention to, and the ones we're not interested in or tend to ignore are the same ones who pay us too much attention. The "attract-repel" that's going on sparks a challenge in us and we tend to want what we can't have. Play it cool and you will be more attractive.

Here are some ideas that will help keep your new flame interested in the new relationship, long past the first few dates:

- Give them time and space. Sure, you want to be with that special person as much as you can. But if he or she takes up too much of your time, you'll get behind in your other commitments, and resentment can easily set in. I suggest going out on dates once or twice a week. Have fun getting to know each other, but remember you have a life outside of him or her.
- Don't give the impression that you're obsessed; that never ends well for anyone.
- If you want the connection to grow, then flexibility is key. If a date is planned that you cannot make, then suggest an alternative.
- Save the gift giving for when you know your new mate is the one for you. Sure, it's okay to purchase small tokens of appreciation. But lavish gifts should be saved until you know you're with the right one.

Growing Together

Probably the hardest thing to do at the start of a relationship is to be yourself. You know your flaws and your tendencies, and you don't want to do anything that will turn the other person off. But here's something important to remember: He or she was attracted to you – not the person that you think you need to be. So relax from the start. Don't pretend to be someone you're not as this will eventually backfire. No false advertising!

When you're on those early dates, this is the best time to be clear about your goals and the way you see life. Honesty and communication is key. Be clear about your likes and your dislikes, and be sure to evaluate where the other person is coming from. For instance, make sure you both share similar core values and the same goals. If you desire to own a house on a quiet street in the suburbs and he or she is set on living in a downtown condo, one of you will have to make a really big lifestyle change. Are you willing to make this change? Is he or she?

Example: *My friend Sandra and her hubby Fab have been married and together for nineteen years now. They started out very slow, but were always very committed to each other. They both had a life outside of their relationship, and were both accepting of each other's time. Fab was the handsome guy who enjoyed going out with the boys. I would tell her the reason Fab stayed with her was because she didn't bust his balls all the time, questioning why he had to go out with his friends. She was easygoing, nurturing, kind and always looked good – and still does to this day. They dated ten years before marrying, and as much as she wanted that ring she never bugged him about it. She let him propose when he was ready. Nine years later they are still together, madly in love, with two kids.*

The Texting Game

*Y*our phone buzzes. You pull it out and you've got a new text message. You smile and text back, and put your phone away – while hoping you'll get another text soon. But when the next text comes, you're puzzled; why did he say that? Why did she respond that way? What do you do next?

Texting is so common early in a relationship, but there is such a thing as texting etiquette. Things like when to text, when to call someone, or how many texts are too many need to be addressed.

Texting has really changed the already complicated dating scene, and one bad text can potentially kill a developing relationship. Smart phones have certainly made communicating with potential partners easier, but understanding text etiquette is crucial if you want to avoid minor oversights that will crumble your world.

Here are some things you will want to consider when swapping mini-missives with your partner.

Texting Pointers

If you had an amazing date, then send a text the next day and say, "Thank you, I had a great time." If you're more traditional, you may want to call – a call is always more personal – but do what you feel is most comfortable. You want to, and need to, make the other person feel special, plus a quick note is common and welcomed courtesy. Simply let them know you enjoyed their company. Just don't do so in a stalking kind of way, like: "When are we going out again?" Avoid asking questions, and don't be intrusive, and call or text to push him or her into another date.

Texting has really changed the already complicated dating scene, and one bad text can potentially kill a developing relationship.

If you are texting someone, *send them a real message.* Don't just say "HI." Hi what? That's just annoying. How is someone supposed to respond to "HI?"

Texting is part of today's dating game, and you really need the correct strategy to get it right. No matter how much you hate it, you have to engage at the beginning of a courtship. That whole, "What do I do?" "What do I say?" "Do I wait for them to call or text?" "Do I reply right away?" is enough to drive a person mad.

If someone you like texts you, don't go two or three days without texting back. Respond within a few hours. Avoiding sending a text isn't an option; don't "play games" with someone you are interested in. You'll lose out. Remember, if you haven't met this person yet and you are texting back and forth, this is not game playing because you haven't established face-to-face chemistry yet. They are not texting you back right away because they are probably busy and you are not their priority.

However, if you have no interest, do what you want to. You have nothing to lose with a non-response.

What if…?

Text times are also critical in determining someone's intentions. If someone is always flirt texting you past 10 p.m., usually they are scheming a score. If someone can't text you during regular business hours or early evening, they might just want you for sex.

Here's a biggie: *Never* text someone while drunk, unless you know them really well! Intoxicated people get way too excited and they write stupid things. Don't be one of them!

Example: *Anna had been with Corey for about one month when she went on vacation with her friends. While she was away, she was texting Corey constantly. Her intentions might have been good – she only wanted him to know he was on her mind – but alcohol clouded her judgment and she was texting ridiculous things like: "I am in the room with these guys, but none of them compare to you. I don't want it to be them, I want them to be you. I miss you so much."*

By the time she returned, he wanted nothing to do with her. When I asked him why, he told me she blew up his phone. She's supposed to be on vacation; just go on vacation and have fun. She thought she was being all sentimental with messages like: "I miss you so much," and he's thinking: "This girl is nuts. She's on vacation, she's on a beach and she's blowing up my phone!"

FYI, there's an app for that. There are drunk dialing/texting apps that have you sign in when you start drinking and prevent you from calling or texting shortly thereafter, it's not fool-proof, but when the fool is drinking 80 proof, it's usually pretty effective.

You might be one of those people who are so text-savvy that the sound of your phone actually ringing when someone calls you sends you into a state of confusion. If someone takes the time to call you, you *must* call them back. Don't send a return text, otherwise you'll be sending a different message: I'm not interested. And if the other person isn't calling you, then he or she is not making time for you.

Another thing to keep in mind about texting: First dates, and second and third and fourth dates, should not be set up by a text message that says, "So where do you want to go?" If you are genuinely interested in someone, suggest a specific day and time for your date. Instead, say something like: "Hi......., are you free this Saturday? If you're interested, we could grab some lunch downtown. Let me know!"

Pictures Anyone?

You might be wondering, "What about pictures; should I send any via a text?" My advice: Don't start sending sexy pictures in texts before you are in a relationship, otherwise other people may see them. When I first started dating Dean, I sent him photos of myself – fully clothed, no nudes and not in a bikini – and he would show everyone he knew. It is what people do! It wasn't until later that he told me he shared the photos with the guys in his office. I would have been mortified if they were sexy photos!

Ladies, be careful. For instance, another friend of mine used to get half-naked photos from women he met online, and he always shared those pictures with others. It was almost like he was running his own contest for the raciest picture he could get, then celebrating his achievement without any investment. It shocks me on how some women have no self-dignity and can just randomly send nudes or semi-nudes to complete strangers. You know, the picture in the sexy little thong with the side boob, doing the over the shoulder look-back while biting her lip or finger.

Guys, I'm sure it would be flattering to know that the woman you're interested in is bragging about your looks to her girlfriends. But let her show pics of you in stylish clothes, rather than you in boxer briefs with that "come hither" look. It is also for your own safety. If you break up, you may find the picture you thought was sexy attached to an unflattering hashtag on the Internet.

If you are texting someone and don't really like them try to put them into the *friendzone* by saying: "hey there," for a girl, or "hey pal," or "dude" for a guy. A smart person might pick up on this, but some people are totally oblivious. Your best bet: Be upfront, and let the person know that you're only interested in a friendship.

No Obsessing

Texting is certainly something you need to have patience with and show some self-restraint. Someone may not consider messaging you as important; men and women handle situations differently. You might be sitting around waiting, while he or she has something else to do.

Women are more social and spend lots of time gabbing with their many friends. Men, on the other hand, might have one really close friend that he tells everything to. Guys are just not as chatty as women and they are more naturally inclined to communicate through texting.

Don't panic. Don't text and think, "Maybe they didn't get my last text so I'll text again." That's what happens with many people; it is a psychotic thing that goes on in their heads. I once was that person! Most of us go through it when we are younger. You really like someone, or you *think* you really like them, and it is not until you get older that you realize you might have liked them at that time, but you never really knew them. You cannot make a decision about someone until you really know who they are.

So some people get all psychotic and think: "OH MY GOD!" and start obsessing. That's when their behavior turns crazy. A woman thinks, *I am going to go to the bathroom, I'll do my nails, when I come back I'll check my phone and like magic, the text will be there.* Guys, your friends might say, "You want to go for dinner?" And you say, "Yeah, okay.'" But when you are out for dinner, you are constantly on the phone, checking to see if she has texted you. Then you resign yourself to: "It is okay, she will text by the end of dinner…or by the time I get home." Which then becomes, "I wonder if she's okay? I wonder if she even got my message." When you don't hear from him or her for two days, as soon as you receive "the call" or "the text," you ditch your friends for your date. That needy behavior is very unattractive. One way to get over this obsessive behavior is to GET BUSY. Find things you like to do. And try not to overthink what *might* be happening.

Is it possible the two of you are not meant to be together? Sure, but that doesn't mean you're not good enough, attractive enough, or smart enough. That person may not be right for you. Dating and our ability to move forward when things don't work out, is part of the relationship journey.

One way to get over this obsessive behavior is to
GET BUSY.

Let's say you text someone and they do not text you back. It's been a few days. You can send another text and say, "Hey did you get my last text? I haven't heard from you." You never know what could have happened. Maybe she was caught up in a family situation; perhaps he was busy with late hours at work. If your text is not at the top of his or her mind, like it is with you, then it might have been overlooked. And if they don't text – yes there are still plenty of people who don't like to text – then you have got your answer. Let it go. As hard as it may be to understand, if this person is stepping out of your life, it's for a reason. Trust what is happening to you. If this person is not taking the time to call or message you back, they are likely not interested and not the one you're looking for.

In the early stages, if you are the one constantly texting and displaying acts of neediness, that will probably continue throughout the relationship. If you are always asking him or her out, you won't be asked out, because you've set the relationship pattern. We are all creatures of habit, so be careful of the habits you create.

If this person is not taking the time to call or
message you back, they are likely not interested
and not the one you're looking for.

One final note on texting: Auto correct is not always politically correct! Always re-read your texts before pushing send. I swear there are gremlins in phones disguised as auto-correct. They are impish creatures that take a perfectly spelled word, change a letter and sit back and watch all hell break loose.

Section 7

Dating After Divorce

*I*n the world of divorce, there are two types of people:

1.) The divorced person. You feel like you're damaged goods. You feel like a failure when it comes to relationships. And you think everyone views you this way too.

2.) The one considering dating a divorcee. There might have been a time in your life when you felt that dating someone who was divorced was completely unacceptable. The baggage, the drama … the dreaded ex.

In this section, we are going to take an honest look at the one who has been divorced and what he or she can do to move "past their past." It will greatly help the divorceé. It will also benefit the one who is considering dating a divorced person because it will help you understand his or her world so that you can grow together.

A Greater Understanding

While divorce was once unthinkable, today it is considered a socially accepted norm. With almost 50 percent of the married population returning to the singles pool following break up, daters should never dismiss the possibility of dating a divorced individual. If you take the divorced individual out of the equation, you are eliminating a big chunk of potential daters – especially for men and women over 35. The great thing about these people is they tend to be more mature when in relationships.

A failed marriage does not necessarily equate to a bad person. Maybe the two individuals were not really compatible. Perhaps they married under adverse circumstances. Was she pregnant? When he was young, did he give into Mom's words: "Oh she's perfect for you." Perhaps there were simply too many obstacles to overcome. Hopefully, he or she has learned from their mistakes.

Women, take note: Divorced men with children tend to be more mature, mentally and emotionally, than their single, no-kid counterparts. They are also more likely to commit and have most often learned from their first marriage. For instance, Dean is divorced, and I see a huge difference between him and the other guys I used to date.

We All Make Mistakes

Instead of dwelling on the past, and failed relationships, understand that dating after divorce can be as exhilarating as it was when you were nineteen. Except life is better now because you have a stable career, your own home and hopefully some disposable income.

Yes, dating after divorce could potentially be a great life experience. But first, take some alone time. Rather than dive head first into the dating scene, ease yourself into it s-l-o-w-l-y. What I said in an earlier chapter bears repeating: If you are recently divorced, take adequate time to be single and discover what makes you fulfilled and content, and embrace new experiences. The extra alone time will prepare you mentally and emotionally for new relationships.

Immediately after your divorce you might be emotional and feel lonely. That's you adjusting to a new lifestyle. Resist the urge, if you can, to immediately find a shoulder to cry on in the form of a romantic partner. You are stronger than you might think. And loneliness is a perception. You are not alone, you are free. Free to move forward and begin the great next chapter of your life.

Rather than dive head first into the dating scene,
ease yourself into it s-l-o-w-l-y.

A word of caution to men: Many of you are jaded because your ex-wife or former girlfriend has taken you to the cleaners. However, *all* women are not the same. If one woman cheated you financially, that does not mean the next one will. Make sure you don't lead with your cash. Ask yourself: "What have I learned? Did I miss any warning signs? What could

I have done differently?" It is time to embark on the wonderful journey that is dating after divorce only when you are truly ready to move on.

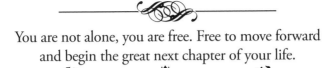

You are not alone, you are free. Free to move forward
and begin the great next chapter of your life.

Taking Inventory

As a divorcee, it can be hard to love yourself while being inundated with societal and cultural expectations of what's "perfect" or acceptable. Oftentimes we lose sight of who we really are and what we're capable of because we are too busy chasing someone else's dream. We stop loving ourselves the moment we forget we're good enough just being the person we are.

No one can be you.

So how do we get back to self-love? Have you forgotten how to love yourself?

First, take a good look at your attitudes about life, about relationships, and about yourself. Remember, it's your attitude that ultimately determines if and how you succeed in life. Take an active interest in feeding your brain with positive information – having a positive attitude is what sustains you when we are going through tough times. If we can develop a positive outlook on the way we see and do things, it can lead to a greater sense of well-being.

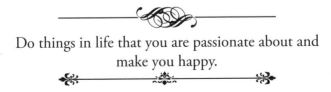

Do things in life that you are passionate about and
make you happy.

Do what you love. Are you in a career or job that brings you joy? If not, do you have daily activities or hobbies that give you satisfaction and fulfillment? Do things in life that you are passionate about and make you happy. Learn to live life to its fullest and enjoy as much of it as possible. Embrace life and all that it has to offer. Set yourself some goals and go after them!

Get to know who you are. To become more comfortable with your forthcoming dating pool, another little trick I suggest is dating yourself. Take yourself to dinner, a movie or try a new sport. The first time you try this you might feel "weird" and think everyone is staring at you. That is not the case. In fact, anyone staring at you may actually have an interest in you.

Try new things, such as a solo vacation – yes, I mean by yourself – and get to know who you really are. Imagine the excitement of travelling alone. You'll be free from distractions, mind-numbing conversations and you'll enjoy some peace and quiet. What better way to familiarize yourself with who you truly are. It takes courage to grow up and accept your life as it is, and to move on to a better one.

Thankfulness and a grateful heart are two of the
best ways to bring peace and healing to your life.

Talk to strangers. Explore the world and new cultures. Try new activities. Find what you are good at. When you do these things, you will learn how to love and understand yourself better, which builds confidence. *Here's a great tip:* Give your time and energy to a nonprofit organization. Yes, volunteer! There is nothing as fulfilling as giving to someone who cannot repay you. Volunteering will help you realize how little some people have and how much you do have. It is another great way to expand your social circle and you may meet another great person interested in meeting someone like you. Love can strike at any time. Thankfulness and a grateful heart are two of the best ways to bring peace and healing to your life.

Take a Look Around

Who are you presently connected to? What relationships lift you up or drag you down? I encourage you to accept only healthy/positive relationships in your life and surround yourself with people who complement you, or challenge you in a positive way. Remember, the people in your world are a true reflection of your level of love for yourself. What are you willing to put up with? What behaviors do you accept from others? Are you willing to cut out or distance yourself from toxic relationships that have never served you any purpose, other than to heap guilt and condemnation on you?

Taking time to reflect on the relationships around you is important to help you stay grounded and bring you back to you. Remember, the lives you are connected to are a true reflection of how you feel inside.

Take care of your body. When I say body, I mean your entire body. This means be conscious of the food you eat, food can have a huge impact on our mood and energy levels. Try a physical activity that is fun for you and that yields the results you are wanting. For some, yoga brings a lot of calm to their lives, while others turn to running to escape life anxiety.

Patience and Self-Talk

Are you patient with yourself when you are having a bad day or not quite where you want to be? Being impatient is born out of anxiety. Anxiety is oftentimes brought about by comparing yourself with others, which perpetuates the "grass is always greener" effect. Your life is your own. Embrace the *now*; embrace where you want to be and spend every day making strides towards your goals. Trust when you need to be patient on that path, that your life is a journey, and that journey is about becoming a fantastic, unique evolution of you.

Have you heard of the term "self-talk"? It is the inner monologue that goes on 24/7 in our minds. It is said that most people speak at a rate of 150 to 200 words per minute, and the mind can listen to about 500-600 words a minute. However, our self-talk goes at a rate of up to 1,300 words per minute! Our self-talk is a true reflection of our beliefs and values; it is the "filter" through which we determine what we like and don't like.

The most important person in your life is you.
It all starts and ends with you.

If you want to truly begin to change the way you think and act towards yourself – and others – then I challenge you to get in tune with your self-talk. What are you saying about yourself? About others? Here is a truth: Beliefs direct thoughts, thoughts direct feelings, and feelings determine actions and reactions. Now, how do you treat yourself? How do you talk to yourself? If you are hard on yourself, you can transition by changing what you believe and think about yourself. You can learn to be gentle with yourself, to be patient and kind. We can be our biggest, and worst, critics. How to love yourself starts with you. So determine that you are going to change at least one belief and thought that you have about yourself. Do this weekly and in no time you'll have a completely different outlook on yourself – and life!

Never forget, the most important person in your life is you.

It all starts and ends with you.

The Haunting Ex

If you are entering the dating pool after divorce, you have to know that rules of dating have changed dramatically since you were single. One of the biggest no-no's you must grasp quickly is to *leave your ex in the past!*

Dating is not a substitute for counseling. If you cannot do this, then you are not ready to date. And if you start relating everything that happened in your marriage to your current date, you will send him or her running for the closest EXIT sign.

However, if your ex does come up in conversation, don't speak negatively; doing so will only make you look like the angry type, the pouting type, or the woe-is-me type. This is a huge turnoff, and a clear indication that you are not ready to date.

Example: *Christina met Marek online. They texted back and forth, then she asked him to give her a call. As she puts it, she likes the three-dimensional people. Christina likes to talk to the other person, and hear his voice before she goes out with him, to get an idea of what he sounds like and see if he can carry on a conversation. However, they weren't able to connect on the phone prior to meeting. Against her better judgment, she decided to meet him anyway. (This can happen when you've been dating for so long, with no luck, and you just want to meet someone.)*

Christina was already seated at the restaurant when Marek came in. He sat down, with no smile and a little shorter than he described himself. (This is one of the big things that guys lie about on their profile.) She said, "Hi nice to meet you. How was your day?"

He then told her to hold on as he needed to read the menu first. It was then that his thick accent came through loud and clear.

They were both looking over their menus in awkward silence. He had his menu pulled up to his face, so Christina couldn't read his facial expressions. Marek finally put the menu down and said, "We are good" to which she replied how was your day? She could hardly understand him due to his accent. And getting any conversation going was painful.

When Christina asked him if he had any siblings, he burst into a diatribe about his ex-girlfriend and how they had just broken up because they weren't getting along. Christina found this confusing; was he dating his sister? She didn't want to ask because he was well worked up by now. He told her that his ex/sister, whatever, texted him one day and said, "I'm in Vegas and I'm on my own now," because he wasn't paying attention to her anymore. Christina tried to be patient and sympathetic, but instead, she decided to be a smarty pants, she said, "Oh boy you must have pissed her off."

At that point, he became defensive and said, "I didn't do anything wrong. Is it my fault that I have to work to pay bills?" He went on and on about his ex sending scandalous pictures of herself with other men, which made him want to go find her, but he didn't know where she was staying.

Basically, Christina was a therapist that night.

When the bill mercifully came, she reached for her wallet to split the cost. Instead, he said he would pay, then she could go to the bank machine and pay him her half. Talk about strange! He even walked her to the machine. Needless to say, that was the first and last time they saw each other. Ladies, this type of situation warrants you to pretend you're going to the bathroom and make a quick exit out the front or back door, whichever is closest!

Baby Talk

Other than saying you have children, refrain from going into too much detail. The first few dates are about you and your potential new partner. While kids are such an important part of life, your focus should be on discovering mutual interests and ways that you connect. Does she make you laugh? How does he carry himself in public? Does he or she strike you as genuine, or carefully guarded. Get to know more about who he or she is before you share information about your children.

However, if you both have children, they are common ground, and parents can certainly relate to one another on this level. But save the heavy topics for later.

Relationships are always more enjoyable when two people genuinely connect as friends.

Have fun and keep it light on the first few dates. Talk about your interests, hobbies, books you have read or movies you have watched (hint, refer back to the conversation starters on page 148). Let the individual know what sets you apart from the rest – make it clear that a life with you would be fun and adventurous!

Relationships are always more enjoyable when two people genuinely connect as friends. Sure, you may feel chemistry and even sexual connection with the new person in your life. If you've been divorced for a while, it is tempting to jump head first into a relationship that you've been longing for. Make sure the two of you are really compatible before you fully commit body and soul. And please, don't rush into a second marriage even if you think this person is the epitome of perfection (trust me, he/she has flaws.) Years of being married may compel you to convince yourself that you should tie-the-knot again, ASAP.

I say wait.

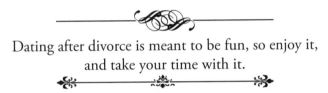

Dating after divorce is meant to be fun, so enjoy it,
and take your time with it.

Or perhaps you both have children and there is no real need to get married again. After all, you are content living in common law and are just as happy without a marriage certificate.

If your relationship is as wonderful as you think it is, you can certainly wait a year or two. You have been married before so what is the rush? If someone you have been dating for less than a year gives you the marriage ultimatum, they may not have the best intentions in the first place. Don't give into such an unfair demand. Dating after divorce is meant to be fun, so enjoy it, and take your time with it. Make your next relationship a successful one!

Break the Cycle

Have you ever wondered why you keep picking the wrong partner? Are you continually attracting bad boys/girls, unstable partners who are irresponsible in their personal or financial lives?

Why do people keep picking the wrong partner? It could stem from unresolved childhood issues. As an adult, you are still suffering from traumatization that could be called "daddy or mommy issues." I'm not being factious; this is a fact of life for many adults.

Growing up, my father wasn't always the hands-on type, and he wasn't the cuddling, "you are doing well" male I needed (my primary love language is physical touch and secondary language is words of affirmation). I look at the relationship he had with my mom and it wasn't a very satisfying one. No doubt seeing their dysfunctional relationship greatly impacted my relationships with men.

This kind of thing is very common. I see the same things with a friend; her dad wasn't always around. He was too busy cheating on her mom before their divorce. These childhood experiences left her wounded – she has always had abandonment issues – so she keeps choosing the same type of relationships.

I encourage you to find forgiveness for those who
have hurt you in the past.

If you recognize that your childhood has had a negative impact on your adult life, I encourage you to get some help and work through your issues. You can't continue to blame others for what you have been through in the past. As an adult, you must come to the place where you realize that your parents and their relationship do not have to be projected into your current relationships. Either talk to a professional or figure it out with a good friend; this is not something you should do yourself. I encourage you to find forgiveness for those who have hurt you in the past. When you find your way to forgiveness, you will be amazed by the profound changes in your life.

CONCLUSION

*E*very weekend morning when I wake, Dean has a freshly brewed cup of coffee waiting for me. I know that he's a man of integrity, he has my back, and he makes me feel secure. It's things like these that make me love Dean more each day. Since we've been together, I've realized how much he has helped me as a dating/matchmaking expert. He has shown me what a close-to-perfect person truly is, and it is my goal to help single people everywhere to find the perfect person for them!

There is someone out there for everyone!

As you journey through your dating world, I encourage you to embrace all that the single life has to offer. Revel in your independence. Enjoy the lack of relationship stress. You have the freedom to do whatever you want, when you want. Don't rush and compromise to find the right relationship for you. Remember, it's better to be single wishing you were married than married wishing you were single.

There is someone out there for everyone! So keep trying. Sometimes you may need to take a break from dating, but once you are ready, get back out there with a positive frame of mind. Dating can be tough and you're not the only one going through the struggles of meeting the "right one." If you were, a lot of magazines and therapists would be out of business!

I was single for three years before I met Dean, and I have friends who have been single for longer than that. Everything I went through during those three years of being single is what brought Dean into my life; the good, the bad and the ugly, but if it weren't for those lessons, I'd probably still be doing laps in the dating pool.

The best thing you can do for yourself is to make a goal of always bringing your best version forward. This will result in attracting Mr. or Ms. Right; it has to, it's the Universal Law.

When you're the best version of yourself, you will enjoy and appreciate your own company and being single won't matter; although I suspect when that happens, you won't be single for long.

Throughout this book, I've given you my best advice. But I'm still here for you! If you need a little coaching or matchmaking help, contact me at:

laura@singleinthecitydating.com

laura@singleinthecity.ca

or
singleinthecitydating.com or singleinthecity.ca

BONUS SECTION

Go to http://singleinthecity.ca or singleinthecitydating.com for a free download - People to Avoid So You Don't Waste Your Time on Dead End Dates and Relationships.

ABOUT THE AUTHOR

Laura Bilotta is a leading, prominent dating coach and matchmaker, with an earned reputation throughout North America. She founded Single in the City fifteen years ago, and since then has used her highly developed and intuitive skills to successfully unite thousands of singles through her singles events and matchmaking services.

As a dating coach, she provides individuals with critical tools to successfully navigate the complex dating world. Laura also hosts her own television show, Single in the City, and is a frequent source of advice for reputable media brands in North America.

Laura shares her life with her devoted boyfriend of five years and her twelve-year-old dog, Max. Together they live in a quiet suburb just outside of Toronto.